BUZZ NUMBERS

The Explanations and Regulations Behind America's Military Aircraft Identification System

Peter M. Bowers
David W. Menard

specialtypress
PUBLISHERS AND WHOLESALERS

Published by
Specialty Press Publishers and Wholesalers
39966 Grand Avenue
North Branch, MN 55056
United States of America
(800) 895-4585 or (651) 277-1400
www.specialtypress.com

Distributed in the UK and Europe by
Midland Publishing
4 Watling Drive
Hinckley LE10 3EY, England
Tel: 01455 254 450 Fax: 01455 233 737
www.midlandcountiessuperstore.com

ISBN-13 978-1-58007-103-1
ISBN-10 1-58007-103-1

Printed in China

Cover Main:
This North American P-51D-25-NT 44-72948 provides a classic view of a classic aircraft. (Colonel F. Bamberger)

Title page:
North American AT-6F 44-81870 caught in the act of buzzing Coraopolis Army Air Field, Pennsylvania, in March 1946 and displaying the tail number very clearly under its left wing. (William J. Balogh Sr.)

Back Cover:
Top:
North American P 51Ds in the upper photo display their pre June 1948 Buzz Numbers. Both 873 (with smaller digits) and 926 have had replacement rudders installed. (USAF)

Middle:
North American F 51Ds of an Air Force Reserve unit display the post June 1948 Buzz Numbers, including three from the photo above as well as red/white trim on their noses, wing, and fin tips. (USAF)

Bottom:
This chance photo caught an F 100D and an F 100F on the 354th TFW with the same "last three" taking off together. Notice their Buzz Numbers FW 774 and FW 774A. (F Street)

Table of Contents

	Dedication	4
	Introduction	4
	Acknowledgments	4
Chapter One	Before the Buzz Number System	5
Chapter Two	Buzz Number System	12
Chapter Three	Fighters	17
Chapter Four	Bombers	26
Chapter Five	Cargo & Transport	30
Chapter Six	Pursuit	35
Chapter Seven	Trainers: Dedicated	39
Chapter Eight	Trainers: Adapted	44
Chapter Nine	Liaison	47
Chapter Ten	Miscellaneous:	51
	Amphibians	51
	Attack	52
	Photo	53
	Gliders	55
	Utility	58
	Target	58
Chapter Eleven	Three-Letter Buzz Numbers	59
Chapter Twelve	U.S. Air Force	61
Chapter Thirteen	National Insignia	63
Chapter Fourteen	Miscellaneous Colors	65
Chapter Fifteen	Air National Guard	69
Chapter Sixteen	Errors and Oddities	72
Appendix One	T.O. 1-1-81 11 June 48	78
Appendix Two	AFR 65-60 11 June 48	78
Appendix Three	AFR 65-60 9 May 49	81
Appendix Four	T.O. 07-1-1	84
Appendix Five	T.O. 1-1-81 15 August 55	85
Appendix Six	T.O. 1-1-636 11 January 56	87
Appendix Seven	T.O. 1-1-4	89
Appendix Eight	AFR 66-11 18 September 62	90
Appendix Nine	Teletype Message (TWX) 24 April 72	94
Appendix Ten	National Aircraft Insignia Layout	95

Dedication

This book is dedicated to Peter M. Bowers, who helped set the standards for aviation photography and accurate aviation writing. Pete's generosity in both loaning photographs and negatives from his vast collection and in offering advice on how best to present the history of aviation subjects knew no bounds. He took time to answer letters from anyone who contacted him. His shoes will never be filled.

Introduction

About 10 years ago, Pete and I started gathering material for a book covering the U.S. Air Force Buzz Number system that existed from 1945 to 1964. We decided to also include the several aircraft designation changes that occurred in those 19 years, plus some explanations of other U.S. Air Force markings before both of our corporate memories were gone. With Pete's unfortunate passing in April 2003, it remained up to me to finish up our work as best I could. I hope this effort measures up.

Actual pages from *USAF Regulations and Technical Orders* are included as appendices so readers can see for themselves the reasons for certain markings and designations. Hopefully these prove once and for all what it all meant and when they came into use.

Finally, we decided to include the official (and correct!) layout instructions for the U.S. national insignia. This is the number one mistake that is made on restored U.S. military aircraft.

Acknowledgments

Aeronautical Systems Center History Office
William J. Balogh Sr.
Brian R. Baker
Colonel Fred Bamberger, U.S. Air Force, Retired
Roger F. Besecker
Warren Bodie
Peter M. Bowers
Larry Davis
Archie DiFante (AFHRA)
Robert Esposito
Roger A. Freeman
Technical Sergeant Marty J. Isham, U.S. Air Force, Retired
Keith Laird
William T. Larkins
Al Lloyd
Paul M. Paulsen
Victor D. Seeley
Paul D. Stevens
Lieutenant Colonel B. C. Reed, U.S. Air Force, Retired
Jeannette Remak
Maj. Eugene Sommerich, U.S. Air Force, Retired
Lieutenant Colonel Stan Staples, U.S. Air Force, Retired
Technical Sergeant Norman E. Taylor, U.S. Air Force, Retired
Charles Trask
U.S. Air Force Museum
Gordon S. Williams

BEFORE THE BUZZ NUMBER SYSTEM

Curtiss R-4s from 1916. Number 187 is the Army's 187th aircraft. The red star on the rudder (repeated under the wings) was adopted by the Army at the time of the Mexican Punitive Expedition of 1916. (Signal Corps)

The famous identification system for U.S. Army and U.S. Air Force aircraft from late 1945 into the mid-1960s, the "Buzz Number" system, was a combination of two preceding identification systems, one of which is still in use.

Individual Aircraft Serial Numbers

Ever since the U.S. Army began operating aircraft in 1909, individual examples within the service have been identified by a sequential Army serial number, starting with one, painted large on the vertical tail or on the side of the fuselage.

Into 1918, the serial number was sometimes preceded by the letters S.C., for Signal Corps, since Army Aviation at that time was a branch of the Signal Corps. After the U.S. Army Air Service was established on 20 May 1918, the letters were changed to A.S. for Air Service, but these were mostly seen after the war. The prefix letters A.C. for Air Corps were adopted when the Air Service became the Air Corps on 2 July 1926.

The sequential serial number system continued into calendar year 1921. It topped out at 68592, with a special block ranging from 94014 through 94112. The high numbers up to 68592 were the result of thousands of aircraft ordered during World War I, with many being canceled after the Armistice.

Fiscal Year Serial Numbers

At the start of the government's fiscal year 1922 (1 July 1921 through 30 June 1922), a new serial number system for individual aircraft identification was adopted.

Sperry M-1 22-1 was the very first Army aircraft to use the new fiscal year system of serial numbers. (USAF)

This was based on the number of aircraft procured within a particular fiscal year. The first one applied was 22-1, to the first Army aircraft ordered in fiscal 1922. This system, still in use, is based on the World War I German system of identifying the numbers of a particular type of aircraft procured within a particular calendar year.

The markings FOK D.VII #7775/18 stenciled on the side of a German aircraft meant that it was a Fokker, the seventh Fokker D-model or fighter, and the 7775th overall D model procured in 1918. The highest fiscal year serial number ever assigned to a U.S. Army aircraft was 42-110188, a Consolidated B-24J-140, ordered during World War II.

From the early 1920s through World War II, aircraft assigned to training schools were usually identified by large individual fuselage numbers within that base's inventory, rather than by their Army serial number.

Serial Number Display

With the exception of the combat squadrons in the American Expeditionary Force (AEF) in France in World War I, the serial numbers of U.S. Army aircraft were displayed on each side of the fuselage in sizes diminishing from 12 inches down to 4 inches by the end of 1926. In 1927, the make and model of the aircraft, as well as the letters U.S. ARMY, were added to the serial number on the fuselage.

In 1932, this conspicuous and convenient display was abandoned, and the service designation, model number, and serial number were condensed into 1-inch stenciled figures in a Data Block on the left side of the fuselage near the cockpit. It remained here until the 1990s, when it was reduced to 1/2-inch figures near the ground refueling receptacle.

New Tail Numbers

The need to identify individual aircraft from a greater distance was recognized in 1941. The 28 October 1941 revision to Army Air Forces Technical Order 07-1-1, "Aircraft Camouflage, Markings, and Insignia," called for an abbreviated form of the Army serial number to be painted on each side of the vertical tail. However, the numbers did not appear on the aircraft until after Pearl Harbor and well into January 1942. The correct name for

Stearman PT-13s lined up at Randolph Field, Texas, in 1938 with their large field numbers on their fuselages. Since no radios were carried, no radio call numbers were displayed. (USAF)

Vultee BT-13As from Moffett Field, California, displaying their base identification numbers, using the first letter of the base name plus the field number. (USAF)

Curtiss P-3A 28-191 displaying the three-line identification on its rear fuselage. The smaller stenciling just forward of the cockpit is the Technical Data Block, which contains weights, fuel, armament, and rigging data. (Bowers Collection)

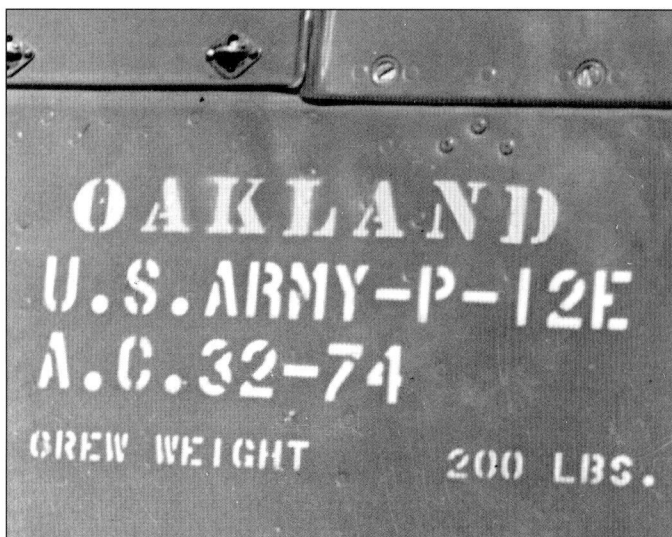

The Technical Data Block moved to its new location near the cockpit on the left side of the fuselage. (Bowers Collection)

The Controversial "O" Prefix

In the years after World War II, many U.S. Air Force (established as a separate branch of the U.S. armed forces on 18 September 1947) aircraft exceeded a decade of service. To avoid conflict between identical tail numbers issued 10 years apart, the prefix letter O (oh), not 0 (zero), followed by a dash was added to the tail number (radio call number) of the earlier aircraft. This was to indicate "Over 10," but some believe "O for Obsolete" is more appropriate. The application is clearly spelled out in the 20 July 1954 revision to T.O. 07-1-1, and is quoted verbatim here:

"Where aircraft are ten years old, there is a possibility that two sets of call numbers could be identical. To prevent this, the symbol 'O' precedes radio call numbers derived from serial numbers which are ten years old." (Please see Appendix 6 for a reproduction of this page from the T.O.)

This requirement was dropped in April 1972 for reasons unknown. (Please see Appendix 9 for a reproduction of the TWX sent to the field on this subject.)

Boeing B-17E 41-2399 displays the correct format for the serial number used as the radio call (tail) number by dropping the 4 and dash and placing the 1 into it. (Bowers Collection)

these numbers on the tail is "radio call numbers," but we use the more familiar term "tail number" in this book.

For example, the fiscal year serial number for Boeing B-17E 41-2399 was applied to the tail without the first digit of the fiscal year or the dash as "12399." The full serial number could not be fitted on the fins of small aircraft, so it was applied to the sides of the fuselage. If the serial number was short, such as 41-2 or 43-37, the tail number was expanded to a minimum of four digits by inserting zeros to get 1002 and 3037. At the time, there was no problem anticipated in eliminating the decade digit; it simply made for a shorter number. Military aircraft were not expected to last more than 10 years, so no conflict with a later 51-2399 was anticipated. About 1956, the minimum digits to be displayed in the radio call number expanded to five digits. For instance, B-52H-125-BW 60-1 displayed 00001 on her fin.

Boeing XB-29 41-2 had its radio call number expanded to the mandated minimum four digits by inserting some zeros to make it 1002. (G. S. Williams)

Unit Aircraft Identification

Starting with the AEF squadrons in France in 1918, U.S. Army aircraft were identified as to squadron by distinctive squadron insignia applied to each side of the fuse-

Convair F-106A-105-CO 59-7 of the 319th Fighter Interceptor Squadron displays her FE-007 Buzz Number and 90007 tail number. (Lieutenant Colonel W. Gatschet)

lage. Individual aircraft within the squadron were identified by large block numbers on the fuselage and sometimes on the wings. In the AEF, the Army serial number of American-built aircraft was painted in small figures at the top of the rudder. Aircraft obtained from the Allies used that country's serial number and locations. The squadron identification system by insignia continued until the United States entered World War II. Earlier, however, starting in 1937, the system was modified to identify Army aircraft visually by group as well as by squadron.

A new marking called a designator was added to the vertical fin and to the upper and lower surfaces of the left wing. This appeared on the fin as two letters above a number. The first letter identified the group as to type—P for pursuit, B for bomber, etc. The second letter was rather illogically used to identify the numbered unit by still another letter. A combination such as PA was easy to identify as the First Pursuit Group, "A" being the first letter of the alphabet. On the other hand, a combination like PT took a bit of figuring to determine that "T" was the 20th letter of the alphabet and therefore identified the 20th Pursuit Group. The number below the letters was the individual aircraft number within the group, not the squadron. Squadron insignia and colored noses continued to identify the squadrons within the group until after Pearl Harbor.

For 1940 and 1941, the group designator system was revised to use a more logical number to identify the already numbered group. Aircraft of the 35th Pursuit Group were now identified by the line "35P," and the aircraft number within the group was placed above the group designator.

The British System

When the Eighth Air Force of the Army Air Forces began operations in England in 1942, it adopted the prevailing British system of using two large letters (or letters and numbers) on the side of the fuselage to identify the squadron, and a separated single letter to identify the individual aircraft within the squadron. This British system was used for operations in the European theater of operations (ETO) and to some extent in North Africa and

Continued on page 11

Boeing B-52H-125-BW 60-1 displays Technical Order perfect application of her radio call number. (M. Isham via D. Logan)

Curtiss P-36A from Selfridge Field, Michigan. The P in the tail designator was for pursuit, the A for First Fighter Group, and 91 was the plane in unit number. This was repeated on the top and bottom surfaces of the left wing as PA 91. (USAF)

This photo shows the need for large format radio call (tail) numbers as no dry report ever could! More than 150 brand new P-40s were in flyable storage at Patterson Field in May 1941, with only a 1-inch black stencil under each left cockpit rail to identify them. Imagine looking for a specific P-40 in this batch. (USAF Museum)

Curtiss P-36A from the 35th Pursuit Group, as indicated by the 35P on the vertical fin. (Bowers Collection)

Boeing B-17G-25-VE 42-97674 displaying the British-style identifiers used by the Eighth Air Force. (USAF)

Italy, but was not adopted for U.S. Army aircraft in other theaters or the continental United States. This system was readable only by ground observers when the aircraft was on the ground, or when taking off and landing. In flight, these markings would be read by other aircraft flying close by at nearly the same level or above. After V-E Day, 8 May 1945, the Eighth Air Force had a need to identify individual flying aircraft from the ground. To meet this need, it added the fuselage lettering to the underside of the left wing, thereby starting the process that led to the development of what came to be called the Buzz Number system.

THE BUZZ NUMBER SYSTEM

Beach T-34A 53-3334 displays only its Buzz Number on the fuselage because of the lack of room for the national insignia. (C. Nelson)

After V-E Day in May 1945, many Eighth Air Force pilots engaged in unauthorized low-level flying over war-ravaged Europe. This practice, called "buzzing," resulted in a need for ground observers to identify and report a particular offending aircraft. To aid them, the Eighth Air Force applied fuselage codes to the underside of the left wing in large easily read figures.

Why the left wing? In the unique American military aircraft marking system, the national insignia were painted on the upper left and lower right wings, so the lower left wing area was available for additional markings.

Actually, the practice of underwing numbers had been applied in the continental United States late in the war on some bombers and transports. Some advanced trainers and fighters used for training had their radio call (tail) numbers applied to the left wing, and sometimes both wings.

This adaptation of the British system was so effective at its purpose that the Army Air Forces adopted a variation of it for use in the continental United States. It was adopted officially on 10 October 45 through a revision of the long-standing Army Air Forces Technical Order (T.O.) 07-1-1B: "Aircraft Camouflage, Markings, and Insignia." In 1956, this became T.O. 1-1-636, and in 1964, T.O. 1-1-4. Further references in this book identify them collectively as "the T.O."

Form

This consisted of two block letters that identified the aircraft as to type and model, such as P for pursuit, and A for the P-38, the lowest-numbered fighter in the inventory. The letters were assigned sequentially to the models of that type that were in the inventory when the system was adopted. The letters were then followed by a dash and the last three digits of the radio call (tail) number. An example as listed in the T.O. was P-38J 42-67126 as PA-126.

Two North American F-51Ds of the 120th Fighter Squadron, Colorado Air National Guard, after a tornado swept across Wold-Chamberlin Field in Minneapolis in July 1951. (Minnesota Air National Guard,)

An Eighth Air Force Mustang shows off the British style squadron code added to the lower left wing after V-J Day. This code is also on both sides of the fuselage. (R. A. Freeman Collection)

Paragraph 17b of Section III, Markings, specified what were officially called identification markings. Because the intended purpose was to enable identification of low-flying aircraft from the ground, they were soon universally referred to as "Buzz Numbers." Later revisions of the T.O. acknowledged this by referring to the markings in parentheses as Buzz Numbers.

Aircraft Assignments

The October 1945 revision to the T.O. listed practically every aircraft that appeared in the Army Air Forces inventory of the time. Whatever individual or committee made up the original list could not have been well informed as to the actual status of some of the aircraft listed. Some were no longer in service and in scrap yards but still on the books, and others were on experimental models that would never reach production status. Still others, like gliders and very heavy bombers, could hardly be expected to engage in buzzing, which was the reason for listing them.

Not all aircraft assigned Buzz Numbers by the T.O. had them applied. Many were still in inventory but in the process of phasing out, such as the Martin B-26 (BE), which was not marked. Most primary and basic trainers were not marked either, because they were on their way out as designated types. Some individual models, like the one-and-only XB-19A (BB), needed no identification aid. They were so large and unique that one would not forget seeing them.

However, other giants that were illogical buzzing candidates, such as the Convair B-26 (BM), were added to later revisions of the T.O. This was an indication that the system was changing from its original purpose of identifying low-flying aircraft to a simple easy-to-use system of individual aircraft identification far superior to a close-up reading of the radio call (tail) numbers. This is confirmed by the removal of the Buzz Numbers from under the wing and their replacement with USAF on all U.S. Air Force aircraft as specified by the 16 July 1948 revision to the T.O. As appropriately marked aircraft phased out, their model letters became available for use on later models. For

Curtiss C-46D-10-CU 44-77624 towing an XCG-10 glider with its radio call number painted in white under both wings. A number this length and small size would be hard to read and memorize. (USAF)

North American P-51D-30-NA 44-74477 displays its rather large call (tail) number under its left wing. (William J. Balogh Sr.)

example, the letter A as first used on the P-38 was later used on the F-94 and then on the Northrop F-5.

Application

The T.O. further specified the size of the figures, a minimum of 8x12 inches and a maximum of 32x48 inches, but there were exceptions in both directions. These were to be under the left wing and on each side of the fuselage. The authors of the T.O. wisely refrained from specifying a particular fuselage location, stating that it would depend on the surface available.

Each aircraft company put these buzz markings in the same location on all models of their aircraft. For instance, Lockheed placed bold figures on the noses of all their F-80, F-94, and T-33 aircraft. North American placed them on the extreme rear of the fuselages on their F-86A, E, F, and H aircraft, but on the noses of their F-86Ds. Republic put them on the noses of all the various models of the F-84s. Someone at the Republic factory kept very close track of them, as the factory also applied suffix letters at the same time, rather than leaving it to the unit to which the aircraft would be assigned.

The location and size used on Northrop's F-89s left much to be desired, but the size and location of the numbers was probably written into the contract, so the company had no choice. The Century Series also had its different locations for these markings, such as the North American F-100 series, which started out on the nose, then moved to the aft section, and finally, on the fuselage over the wing. The McDonnell F-101 carried them on the belly panels. The Convair F-102 had four locations before the position was finalized. The Lockheed F-104 started out with the numbers located on the nose, but they soon moved to the fuselage over the wing's trailing edge. The Republic F-105 has a small application on its nose, while the Convair F-106 was always on the rear of the fuselage.

North American AT-6F 44-81870 caught in the act of buzzing Coraopolis Army Air Field, Pennsylvania, in March 1946 and displaying the tail number very clearly under its left wing. (William J. Balogh Sr.)

Douglas C-47B-40-DK 44-77277, showing where the CD-277 Buzz Number Number has been removed and replaced by the Air Force. (Lieutenant Colonel B. C. Reed)

The fuselage locations vary greatly on some aircraft models, many of which are illustrated in this book. Some models displayed their Buzz Numbers at different locations at the same time in the same unit, and some individual aircraft carried their Buzz Numbers in the different locations on their fuselages at the same time.

Also, the Buzz Number was to take priority over the national star and bars insignia. A note in the T.O. stated that this insignia could be omitted from the fuselage of small aircraft when there was not sufficient room for the Buzz Numbers and the insignia.

To inaugurate the Buzz Number program, paragraph 17b of the basic T.O. 07-1-1 was revised to read as follows:

"*b. IDENTIFICATION MARKINGS
(a) thru (b) as printed
Black or insignia blue or natural metal or overall*

gray aircraft and yellow on black. Then followed the initial listing of aircraft series and their assigned Buzz Symbols."

The following note was added to the 7 June 1946 revision to avoid duplication of Buzz Numbers on the same model aircraft having the same last three digits of their serial numbers:

"*If two or more aircraft of the same model with the same last three digits of their serial are assigned to the same unit/base, letter suffixes will be added to the presentation.*"

For instance, F-51D-25-NA 44-73345 FF-345A and F-51D-30-NA 44-74345 FF-345 of the 120th Fighter Squadron, COLO ANG.

A revision on 26 July 1948 was more specific as to the aircraft required to carry Buzz Numbers. This time, aircraft of the National Guard were specifically exempt. The list of affected aircraft types was also reduced from nine to three.

Republic F-84E-31-RE 51-626 of the 86th Fighter Bomber Wing at Landstuhl Air Force Base, Germany, displaying factory-applied markings, which were really not required at overseas bases. The radio call number has been painted incorrectly in order to display five digits, as on the unit's fiscal year 1949 model Es. (V. D. Seely Collection)

Another revision on 5 November 1948 added the Department of the Army and Military Air Transport Service aircraft to the list of exceptions.

Because of the separation of the new U.S. Air Force from the U.S. Army on 18 September 1947, new markings reflecting this change became the order of the day. The letters USAF (without periods) were to be placed on the lower surface of the left wing and the upper surface of the right wing on all (underlined in the T.O.) U.S. Air Force aircraft except National Guard and Military Air Transport Service aircraft. Further, the words "U.S. AIR FORCE" were to be placed on both sides or the outer sides of the vertical stabilizer and rudder assemblies of fighters, trainers, and light bombers, with the previous exceptions. Helicopters were to have the words on their fuselages. On larger aircraft, such as medium, heavy and very heavy bombers, transports, and search/rescue aircraft, the words "UNITED STATES AIR FORCE" were to be placed on each side of their fuselage.

A revision on 25 November 1952 changed the color of the Buzz Numbers on black painted aircraft from yellow to insignia red. This was a case of officialdom catching up with fact, as photos show that red was being used on black painted aircraft long prior to this date.

Buzz Numbers on the wings gave way to "USAF" (without periods) slowly after the Air Force became a separate service in September 1947. Aircraft in the inventory had their markings changed by the maintainers, while the manufacturers put them on at the factory. Variations were few, with only Bell Aircraft deviating by putting four periods in the "USAF" on the wings of their X-5 aircraft.

Sometime in the spring of 1953, the decision was made to move the small "U.S. AIR FORCE" on the fins and rudders of fighters and trainers to a larger size on the forward fuselage. The "USAF" on the wings gave way to this same marking, thus creating 2 1/2 times the work (4 letters versus 10). This foolishness lasted only for about two years, when common sense returned, and "USAF" on the wings did also.

The entire system was effectively gone by the mid 1960s; the 6 January 1965 revision deleted the page that listed the assigned Buzz Numbers. Aircraft using them either phased out or had these numbers removed after publication of this T.O. The last production U.S. Air Force aircraft to use the Buzz Number was the McDonnell F-4, and these numbers were painted over on the gray/white models that were delivered before being painted camouflage.

FIGHTERS

Using the letter F to identify U.S. Air Force fighter aircraft in June 1948 seems to have been a case of the designation catching up to the change in unit identification that took place six years earlier, in March 1942, when pursuit squadrons became fighter squadrons. After 17 years of the letter F for foto, designating a camera-carrying aircraft, logic finally reared its head and F became the new identifier for such aircraft as the Mustang, Shooting Star, Sabre, etc. This was an easy marking to modify on the aircraft displaying PX-XXX Buzz Numbers, as all the maintainers had to do was remove the right side of the P and shorten the lower bar a bit.

BUZZ NUMBER	MANUFACTURER/MODEL	REMARKS
FA(1)	Lockheed F-38	F-38 out of inventory by June 1948.
FA(2)	Lockheed F-94	
FA(3)	Northrop F-5	
FB	McDonnell F-101	
FC(1)	Convair F-102	
FC(2)	Convair F-106	Original designation was F-102B.
FD	Republic XF-103	Aircraft never built.
FE(1)	Republic F-47	
FE(2)	Convair F-106	
FF	North American F-51	
FG	Lockheed F-104	
FH	Republic F-105	
FJ(1)	Bell F-59	F-59 out of inventory by June 1948.
FJ(2)	McDonnell F-110	Became F-4 in September 1962.
FK	Northrop F-61	
FL	Bell F-63	F-63 out of inventory by June 1948.
FN	Lockheed F-80	Later changed to FT in 1948.
FP	Convair XF-81	Not in inventory in June 1948.
FQ	North American F-82	
FR(1)	Bell XF-83	Not in inventory in June 1948.
FR(2)	North American F-107	FR on factory painting blueprint when author restored U.S. Air Force Museum example.
FS	Republic F-84	
FT	Lockheed F-80	Was FN
FU	North American F-86	
FV	Northrop F-89	
FW	North American F-100	
FX	Lockheed YF-12	Probably unofficial.
FY	North American YF-93, YF-95	Probably unofficial.

Republic F-47N-25-RE 44-89416, a 14th Fighter Group "Jug," cruises over rugged Maine near Dow Field. The Buzz Number was displayed under the cockpit on all F-47s. (USAF)

North American F-51D-30-NA 44-74850, based at O'Hare Field in 1954, was a senior officer's "toy." All of the markings on this aircraft except the stencil on the main gear doors were decals. The location of the Buzz Number on this Mustang was the predominant one for this model. (Menard)

North American F-51D 4744 with its Buzz Number in a position that was rarely used. The complete serial number was not displayed for unknown reasons. It could have been 474744 or 484744. (Menard)

North American F-51H-10-NA 44-74688, displaying the Military Air Transport Service (MATS) "basketball" on its fin; this was the second most used location for the Buzz Number. (Isham Collection)

Northrop F-61B-20-NO 43-8293 of the 325th Fighter (All Weather) Group at rotation point on takeoff. (Lieutenant Colonel S. Staples)

North American F-82G 46-415, displaying the type's only known location. (Bowers Collection)

Lockheed F-80A-10-LO 44-85275 of the 56th Fighter Group displaying the original Buzz Number in the fall of 1948 during the transition to FT. (P. Bowers)

Lockheed TF-80C 48-358 was the third production example of the two-place Shooting Star. It was overall gray and retained the new FT Buzz Number in its factory-applied location in the fall of 1948. (P. Bowers)

Lockheed RF-80A-1-LO 44-85310 of the 363rd Tactical Recon Group retained the pure fighter Buzz Number. (Bowers Collection)

Lockheed RF-80A-1-LO 45-8310, also from the 363rd Tactical Recon Group, should really have the letter A as a suffix to the Buzz Number to indicate that it was the second FT-310 in the unit. (USAF)

Republic F-84G-1-RE 51-767, near the end of her service, with the Buzz Number moved to the aft section and reduced in size. (USAF)

Republic F-84G-1-RE 51-767, nice and shiny shortly after rollout at the factory, has the factory-applied suffix letter A. (Republic)

Republic F-84F-50-RE 52-6854 displays the midfuselage location of the Buzz Number used by most F-84Fs in the training mission. (Norm Taylor Collection)

Republic F-84E-31-RE 51-9576, displaying one of the highest suffix letters seen on any Air Force aircraft anywhere. JATO bottles are attached under the fuselage. (Esposito Collection)

North American F-86A-5-NA 49-1301 displaying the curved font Buzz Number used by the company on all A, E, F, and H models built. (USAF)

North American F-86A-1-NA 49-1301 with the Buzz Number enlarged and moved to the center fuselage, for reasons unknown. (USAF)

North American F-86D-60-NA 53-4032 of the 323rd Fighter Interceptor Squadron displaying its Buzz Number as originally applied by the factory on all D models. The unique North American curved font was also used on the U.S. AIR FORCE on the fuselage. (Major E. M. Sommerich)

North American F-86D-30-NA 51-6035 of the 87th Fighter Interceptor Squadron with standard USAF block figures, after removal of the nose Buzz Number. (C. Koselke)

North American F-86L-45-NA 52-4168 of the Air Defense Command, still with a third location of the Buzz Number and far different location of the national insignia. (Master Sergeant M. Olmsted)

North American F-86D-55-Na 53-600 of the 95th Fighter Interceptor Squadron, with the Buzz Number as far aft as possible. The "Mr. Bones" unit insignia and fuselage-located commander's bands complete the markings. (Isham Collection)

Four F-86Ds of the 456th Fighter Interceptor Squadron show their Buzz Numbers in three locations, with the center top one displaying it twice. (Brigadier General K. Bell)

Northrop F-89D-40-NO 52-1886, displaying pristine factory markings. One can notice the buzz and radio call numbers are the same size. The F-89 was the only fighter with this situation. (P. Paulsen)

Northrop F-89D-15-NO 51-11301 from the 3550th Combat Crew Training Wing, based at Moody Air Force Base, Georgia, displaying the large Buzz Numbers needed because of all the nearby beaches stocked with young women in swimsuits. (USAF)

Northrop F-89D-60-NO 53-2575 of an unknown training unit, displaying her Buzz Number where it should have been all along. (Menard Collection)

Lockheed F-94A-5-LO 49-2496 from Wright Field, displaying the factory-applied Buzz Number. (USAF)

Lockheed F-94A-5-LO 49-2541 of the Second Fighter Interceptor Squadron, 52nd Fighter Interceptor Group, with unit-applied Buzz Number on the stainless steel skin of the aft section. (USAF)

Lockheed F-94B-1-LO 50-867 displays the most common location for this type's unit-applied Buzz Number. (P. Paulsen)

North American F-100A-1-NA 52-5756, the first production Super Sabre, displaying the original Buzz Number location for this type. (North American)

North American F-100D-1-NA 54-2122, with the final location and extensive use of the North American curved font on all visible markings. (North American Aviation)

Lockheed F-94C-1-LO 51-5601 of the 48th Fighter Interceptor Squadron, displaying the new factory-applied Buzz Number size and location. (Menard Collection)

North American F-100A-10-NA 53-1538, after painting over the midfuselage location of the Buzz Number to enable U.S. AIR FORCE to be applied, causing the Buzz Number to be moved to the titanium paneling, where it rapidly scorched off. (Menard Collection)

McDonnell F-101A-1-MC 53-2418, displaying the only location of Buzz Numbers on the Voodoo series. (McDonnell)

Convair F-102A-5-CO 53-1792, displaying the original location of the Buzz Number for this type. (Convair)

Convair F-102A-30-CO 54-1372 with the least used location for this type's Buzz Number. (Menard Collection)

Convair F-102A 56-1317 with the Buzz Number to the right of the U.S. AIR FORCE on both sides of the fuselage, with the U.S. AIR lettering curving down on the left intake. (Menard Collection)

Lockheed XF-104 53-7786 with the original locations for the Buzz Number and national insignia, the latter of which probably quickly burned off. (USAF)

Convair F-102A-20-CO 53-1810, displaying the final location for this type. (Airman First Class Menard)

Lockheed F-104A-20-LO 56-801 displaying the final locations for the Buzz Number and national insignia. (USAF)

Republic F-105B-20-RE 57-5803 from the Air Research & Development Command's Wright Air Development Division, displaying the only location in which Thunderchiefs ever carried their Buzz Number. (Major E. M. Sommerich)

McDonnell F-4C-18-MC 63-7516 displays her Buzz Number on the fuselage. (Besecker Collection)

Convair F-106B-1-CO 57-2514, displaying the only Buzz Number location ever used on this type. (Convair)

McDonnell RF-4C-20-MC 64-1000 was a recon version of the fighter and retained the Buzz Number of a fighter. (Unknown)

Northrop F-5A-15-NO 63-8421 did not display Buzz Numbers very long—camouflage paint covered all of these markings shortly afterward. (Esposito Collection)

Lockheed YF-12A 60-6934 was the last type of Air Force fighters to be assigned a Buzz Number, but it raises the question: Who would buzz anywhere in a Mach 3-plus aircraft? (Bowers Collection)

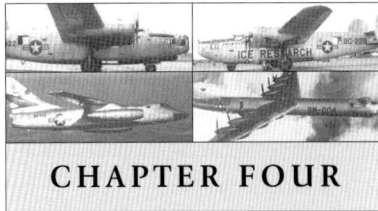

BOMBERS

The letter B for bomber appeared in the first standardized Army Air Service designations of 1920. It paired with other letters that defined the mission, with DB for day bomber, NBS for night bomber short range, etc. The B alone appeared in 1926 and was paralleled by LB for light bomber until 1932.

The original B-for-bomber series reached B-78 in 1958, but the last seven B designations were assigned to unmanned missiles. The manned bomber series started over with the Rockwell (formerly North American) B-1 of 1974.

Heavy bombers were deleted from the Buzz Number requirement by the 1 March 1948 revision to the T.O. The

bombers remaining were considered to be light bombers, so the heading of the column in the T.O. that listed them was changed from bomber to light bomber.

When A-for-attack was deleted in 1947, the only A model then in first-line service, the Douglas A-26 Invader (AC), was reclassified and redesignated as the B-26, so the Buzz Letters changed to BC. There was no conflict with the earlier Martin B-26, because these aircraft were no longer in the inventory. However, it did provide the only case of duplicate Buzz Letters, as there were a few Convair B-24s used in test work into the early 1950s while retaining their BC Buzz Letters.

BUZZ NUMBER	MANUFACTURER/MODEL	REMARKS
BA(1)	Boeing B-17	Deleted March 1948.
BA(2)	Martin B-57	Americanized British Canberra added September 1953.
BB(1)	Douglas XB-19A	Did not get painted on aircraft.
BB(2)	Douglas B-66	Added September 1953.
BC(1)	Convair B-24	Deleted March 1948.
BC(2)	Douglas B-26	Former A-26, added July 1948.
BD	North American B-25	
BE(1)	Martin B-26	None seen with Buzz Number.
BE(2)	North American B-45	Added July 1948; originally BH.
BF	Boeing B-29	Deleted March 1948.
BG(1)	Convair B-32	Deleted April 1947.
BG(2)	Northrop B-35	Added September 1947, deleted July 1948.
BG(3)	Northrop B-49	Not listed in T.O., but did carry that of the B-35, as the B-49 was a conversion of the B-35.
BH(1)	Lockheed B-37	None seen with Buzz Number.
BH(2)	North American B-45	Changed to BE in July 1948.
BJ	Boeing B-39	Reengined B-29. Not seen with Buzz Number.
BK(1)	Douglas B-42	Originally A-42; neither of two known to carry Buzz Number. Deleted April 1947.
BK(2)	Boeing B-50	Added September 1947; deleted 1948, some carried until 1949.
BL	Boeing XB-44	B-29 with R-4360 engines to test for B-50; not seen with numbers.
BM	Convair B-36	Added September 1947; soon deleted but retained until 1949.

Boeing SB-17G-95-DL 44-83710 with full yellow and black Air Rescue markings. Application on the vertical fin/rudder was unusual. (W. T. Larkins photo)

Boeing EB-17G-110-VE 44-85747 with huge Buzz Number on center fuselage over the wing and under left wing, with B suffix indicating there were two other B-17s whose serial number ended in 747. (Bowers Collection)

Martin B-57E 55-4269 towing a target banner. All upper surfaces are painted in insignia orange to assist the shooter aircraft in spotting the tow aircraft to preclude it being shot down. (Bowers Collection)

Convair B-24M-3-FO 44-51922 photographed at Wright Field on 27 June 1947. Another B-24 known to have carried a Buzz Number was 44-41986. (Bowers Collection)

Convair EZB-24M-21-FO 44-51228. This aircraft, the last B-24 on the Air Force roster, was retired in August 1954. After 45 years on display on the Lackland Air Force Base, Texas, parade ground, she was exchanged for a Spitfire from the Imperial War Museum collection in Duxford, England, where she is currently on display. (Bowers Collection)

Douglas RB-66B 53-445's Buzz Numbers on the fuselage are the same size as the radio call number on the fin. (USAF)

Douglas XB-26F 44-34586 displaying the usual position for the Buzz Number on this model. (L. Combs)

North American B-25J-10-NC43-36079 displaying one of the two locations on this model. (P. McDaniel)

North American B-25J-30-NC 44-31327 of the Air Research & Development Command displaying the more common location for the Buzz Number on this model. (Bowers Collection)

North American B-45A 47-063 parked on the Edwards Air Force Base ramp with an insignia red tail. An F-86F, an F-89J, an F-84F, an RF-84F, and an F-102A are parked behind. (Bowers Collection)

Boeing B-29-75-BN 44-62325 of the 96th Bomb Squadron, Second Bomb Group, with the Buzz Number in the other position (versus the nose) on this model. (R. Kamm)

Boeing B-29-40-MO 44-27354 Dave's Dream, a 509th Bomb Group aircraft that dropped the atomic bomb at Bikini Atoll in July 1946. The nose location of the Buzz Number was one of two used by this model. (Georgia Air National Guard photo)

Northrop YB-35 42-102366 carried her Buzz Number in only one location, under the left wing. (Bowers Collection)

Northrop YRB-49A 42-10376 retained her underwing Buzz Number even after application of the U.S. Air Force marking. (Bowers Collection)

North American B-45A 47-011 on a factory test hop, displaying the original BH Buzz Numbers assigned to the B-45 under its left wing as well as on the fuselage. (North American Aviation)

Boeing B-50A-25-BW 46-053 of the Second Bomb Group, displaying the only known location of this model's Buzz Number. (Bowers Collection)

Convair B-36 A-1-CF 44-92004 in a familiar and often used photo of a factory test hop, showing the application of a Buzz Number to the largest aircraft in wing span ever flown by the U.S. Air Force. (USAF)

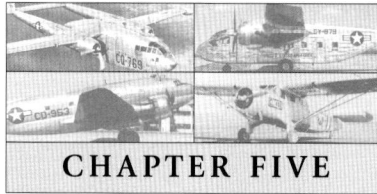

CARGO & TRANSPORT

The letter C has been used continuously from 1925 to the present to identify cargo and transport aircraft. It replaced the previous T, for transport. In October 1942, C models with fewer than eight passenger seats had the letter U for utility added to their C designations.

The Buzz Numbers for the C list in the T.O. started with an oddity, the Beech CQ-3. This was not a true transport, but a director for radio controlled drone aircraft. Since it was the only CQ type in service at the time, but was actually a converted UC-45F, it was logical to give it a cargo plane Buzz Number instead of setting up a one-only CQ list for it.

While many, but not all, of the C models in service between late 1945 and mid-1948 were assigned Buzz Numbers, not all used them. The highest cargo Buzz Number assigned was CZ.

The C models were deleted from the 26 July 1948 revision to the T.O. Buzz Numbers had been assigned to some C models, which were being built but were not completed until the type was exempted. Some others used Buzz Numbers after the deletion date. Because of the short period of use, only two C plane Buzz Numbers were reassigned, and even they were not used.

BUZZ NUMBER	MANUFACTURER/MODEL	REMARKS
CA	Beech CQ-3	Converted from C-45F. Became DC-45F.
CB	Beech UC-43	None seen with Buzz Number.
CC	Beech C-45	
CD	Curtiss C-46	
CE	Douglas C-47	
CF	Douglas C-48	None seen with Buzz Number.
CG	Douglas C-49	None seen with Buzz Number.
CH	Douglas C-53	None seen with Buzz Number.
CJ	Douglas C-54	
CK	Lockheed C-60	None seen with Buzz Number.
CL	Noorduyn C-64	Few seen with Buzz Number.
CM	Lockheed C-69	
CN	Douglas C-74	
CP(1)	Cessna UC-78	None seen with Buzz Number.
CP(2)	Convair C-131	Delivered after deletion from T.O.
CQ	Fairchild C-82	
CR	Convair C-87	None seen with Buzz Number.
CS	Boeing C-97	Only Service test examples used Buzz Number.
CT	Convair XC-99	Delivered too late for Buzz Number.
CU	Douglas C-117	None seen with Buzz Number.
CV(1)	Fairchild C-119	Assigned but never used.
CV(2)	Douglas C-118	Given C-119's CV, not used.
CW	Lockheed C-121	None seen with Buzz Number.
CY	Chase XC-123	Chase CG-20 with P&W R-2800 engines.
CZ	Chase XC-123A	XC-123 fitted with four J47-GE-11 engines.

Beech CQ-3 CA-887, converted from UC-45F 43-35887 for use as a drone director. The CQ designation was short-lived, as CA-887 got redesignated as a DC-45F, with the D prefix identifying it as a drone director. (W. M. Bodie)

The single Curtiss XC-46B was a C-46A-1-CS 43-46953 modified with a stepped windshield and Pratt & Whitney R-2800-34W engines. It is shown here parked on Wright Field. Production C-46Es used this stepped windshield. (Norm Taylor Collection)

Beech C-45E 42-33283 displays the red and yellow markings on its, nose, tail, and wing tips indicating its assignment to the All Weather Flying Center at Clinton County Airport, Wilmington, Ohio. (USAF Museum)

Douglas C-47B-1-DL43-16256 is another rescue-marked aircraft, showing her Army Air Forces markings at an open house. Please notice the word RESCUE and CE-256 in the yellow area just forward of the wing's trailing edge, next to fuselage. (W. T. Larkins)

Douglas SC-47D-45-DK 45-1012 was an odd combination of high-visibility Air Rescue markings over faded and touched-up World War II camouflage. The yellow band covers the center fuselage and wing roots to the ends of the center section. The bands around the rear fuselage and wing tips are also black-bordered yellow, as is the Buzz Number. (W. T. Larkins)

Douglas C-54D-1-DC 42-72443 of the All Weather Flying Center was photographed on 29 June 1947, some six months after the red bar was to have been placed in the center of the rectangles of the national insignia. (Bowers Collection)

Noorduyn UC-64As, such as 44-70444, seldom carried Buzz Numbers. This one, in full Air Rescue markings, has its Buzz Number in a panel on each side of the nose, in the wing root next to the fuselage under the word RESCUE, and centered in the yellow area in the top center of the wing. It also features Buzz Numbers under RESCUE and in the same size as underwing. (L. Sommer)

Lockheed C-69 42-94553, the last C-69 in U.S. Air Force service, was photographed on Wright Field on 27 June 1947, prior to being tested to destruction in nearby Building 65, the Structure Test Facility. (Bowers Collection)

Douglas C-74 42-65404 was one of 14 built of this model and was the first Army Air Force production aircraft to use the mammoth Pratt & Whitney R-4360 engine of 3,500-plus horsepower. (Major E. M. Sommerich)

Fairchild C-119A 45-57769 was an extensively modified C-82A and continued carrying the latter's Buzz Number, even though the C-119 series was assigned CV as its symbol. CQ-769 finished its career at Chanute Air Force Base, Illinois, in the R-4360 engine course. (Fairchild)

This Fairchild C-82A 48-585 was the third-from-last C-82 built. (Fairchild)

Boeing XC-97 43-27472 was photographed at Wright Field on 4 June 1946. (Bowers)

Chase YC-122B 49-2879 was a refined CG-18 glider fitted with Pratt & Whitney R-2000-11 engines. It went on to serve in Tactical Air Command until 1957. (E. Deigan)

Chase XC-123 47-786 was the first of two Chase G-20 gliders fitted with Pratt & Whitney R-2800 engines. Fairchild went on to build the production examples. (Major E. M. Sommerich)

Chase XC-123A 47-787, the first American jet-powered transport, came about when B-47 inboard jet pods with GE J47-11 engines were fitted to the second XC-123. Because of poor performance, no production orders were placed. (E. Deigan)

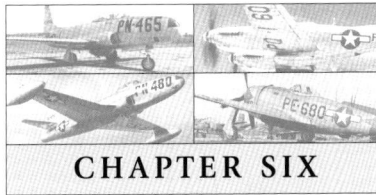

CHAPTER SIX

PURSUIT

The letter P was used from 1920 into 1948 to identify mostly single-seat pursuit aircraft. This was a direct translation of the World War I French term "chasse," or chaser, hence "pursuit." Until 1925, the letter P was paired with other letters to provide other information: PW for pursuit, water-cooled; PG for pursuit, ground attack; TP for two-place pursuit; etc.

With two exceptions, the letter P was used alone from 1925 into 1948. Two two-seat pursuits, the Berliner-Joyce P-16 of 1929 and the Consolidated P-30 of 1933, were redesignated PB-1 and PB-2 in 1934 to identify them as pursuit, biplane.

Seventeen pursuit models were listed in the 1945 T.O., which, in spite of the aircraft's P designations, were listed as fighter aircraft. Only the three pursuit models on the list that had seen combat during World War II continued to serve in squadron strength after the war. Several of the new jet models ordered late in the war attained production in time to carry the P Buzz Number before the change to F. The North American P-86 was the last to be assigned the P Number.

Pursuit aircraft were redesignated as fighters in June 1948. They kept their original model Buzz Number when their symbols were changed from P to F, the P-86 becoming the F-86, etc.

BUZZ NUMBER	MANUFACTURER/MODEL	REMARKS
PA	Lockheed P-38	Very limited post-World War II service. Deleted from T.O. in March 1948.
PB	Bell P-39	No postwar service, none seen with Buzz Number. Deleted in March 1948.
PC	Curtiss P-40	No postwar service, none seen with Buzz Number. Deleted in April 1947.
PD	Curtiss XP-42	Never seen with Buzz Number. Deleted April 1947.
PE	Republic P-47	Kept in service until mid 1950s. To FE in 1948.
PF	North American P-51D/K/H	Kept in service until mid-1950s. To FF in 1948.
PG	Curtiss XP-55	No postwar service, none seen with Buzz Number. Deleted April 1947.
PH	Lockheed XP-58	No postwar service, not seen with Buzz Number. Deleted April 1947.
PJ	Bell P-59	Very limited post-World War II service. Deleted March 1948.
PK	Northrop P-61	Kept in service until late 1940s. To FK in 1948.
PL	Bell P-63	No postwar service. Deleted March 1948.
PM	Fisher P-75	No postwar service, none seen with Buzz Number. Deleted April 1947.
PN	Lockheed P-80	Kept in service until mid-1950s. To FN in June 1948, then to FT.
PP	Convair XP-81	None seen with Buzz Number. Deleted March 1948.
PQ	North American P-82	Kept in service until mid-1950s. To FQ in June 1948.
PR	Bell XP-83	No postwar service. Deleted March 1948.
PS	Republic P-84	On list prior to first flight. To FS in June 1948.
PU	North American P-86	Added April 1947. To FU in June 1948.

This Lockheed P-38L-5-LO 44-53236 is parked at Poplar, Wisconsin, for the Richard Bong Memorial. The aircraft is now painted as one of his aircraft, after a complete restoration by the Minnesota Air National Guard in Duluth. (Esposito Collection)

Republic P-47N-5-RE 44-88680 is a pristine-looking "Jug" of the famous 56th Fighter Group, based at Selfridge Field, Michigan. (Colonel F. Bamberger)

This North American P-51D-25-NT 44-72948 provides a classic view of a classic aircraft. (Colonel F. Bamberger)

The U.S. Air Force Museum was lucky to acquire this Bell P-59B-1-BE 44-22650, one of only a few P-59s that had Buzz Numbers applied. (Major E. M. Sommerich)

North American P-51D-30-NT 45-11654 is a Wright Field Test Pilot School Mustang that displays its Buzz Number in a nonstandard location. (ASC/HO)

Northrop P-61B-20-NO 42-8378 was photographed at a West Coast open house while assigned to an unknown all-weather fighter squadron. (Lieutenant Colonel S. Staples)

This Bell RP-63C-2-BE 43-11074 was painted orange as a manned flying target used to train aerial gunners; it's parked next to an A-26. (Besecker Collection)

The Bell RP-63C-1-BE 45-57300 was an experimental version of a standard overall orange flying target, and may have been redesignated XP-63N. (A. Pelletier Collection)

This Wright Field Flight Test Division Shooting Star, Lockheed P-80A-1-LO 44-85123, won the 1946 Thompson Trophy Jet Race at Cleveland, Ohio. (P. Bowers)

On a combination test flight/photo shoot as a brand new shiny aircraft, Lockheed P-80B-1-LO 45-8480 displays its large Buzz Number under the left wing. (USAF)

Lockheed FP-80A-5-LO 44-85465 should be marked with an F for photo and another second letter instead of the PN for pure fighter, but for reasons unknown, the Air Force went with the fighter symbol. This aircraft won both the 1946 and 1947 Bendix Jet cross-country races from Los Angeles to Cleveland. (P. Bowers)

North American P-82B-1-NA 44-65160. Notice the spaced out underwing Buzz Number permitting it to be seen when carrying external stores. (Bowers Collection)

Republic P-84B-11-RE 45-59551 shows the insignia red tail and outer wing areas designed for visibility in Alaska during cold weather tests at Ladd Field. (Bowers Collection)

North American XP-86 45-59597, the "Daddy of Them All" Sabre, showing off her beautiful lines at Muroc Army Air Field, which later became Edwards Air Force Base. (USAF)

Republic P-84B-36-RE 46-652 flies over Long Island on a combination test flight and photo shoot with another brand new Thunderjet. (Republic)

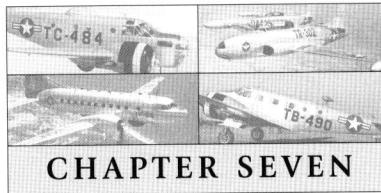

TRAINERS: DEDICATED

Since the letter T was first used to designate trainers, it was always used with another letter until 1948. In 1920, it was paired with other letters to indicate aircraft cooling—TA for trainer, air cooled, and TW for trainer, water cooled.

In 1925 the meaning changed. AT now meant advanced trainer and PT meant Primary trainer. An intermediate training category, BT for basic trainer, was adopted in 1930. All three of these remained in use until 1948, when the category letters were deleted, and all designated trainers became plain Ts.

Exceptions had to be made, however, because of model number duplication. The Vultee BT-13 and Boeing/Stearman PT-13 retained their prefix letters until the aircraft were phased out.

The letter T was also used as a prefix to designations of nontrainer types diverted to specialized training. While all of the AT types in service carried Buzz Numbers, primary and basic trainers, although having them assigned, apparently did not use them.

BUZZ NUMBER	MANUFACTURER/MODEL	REMARKS
TA(1)	North American AT-6	Became T-6 in 1948. LT-6G used in
		Korean War with LTA Buzz Numbers.
TA(2)	Piper PA-18	Unofficially used by civilian flying schools with tie in to civilian registration number.
TB	Beech AT-7	To T-7 in 1948.
TC	Beech AT-11	To T-11 in 1948.
TD(1)	Fairchild AT-21	None seen with Buzz Number. Deleted April 1947.
TD(2)	Beech T-34A	Added September 1953.
TE(1)	Vultee BT-13	None seen with Buzz Number. Deleted October 1949.
TE(2)	Beech T-36	Proposed twin-engined trainer, not built, added to T.O. September 1953.
TE(2)	Cessna T-37	
TF(1)	Stearman PT-13	None seen with Buzz Number. Deleted October 1949.
TF(2)	Northrop T-38A	Added in 1959.
TG(1)	Stearman PT-17	None seen with Buzz Number. Deleted October 1949.
TG(2)	North American T-39	Added in 1959.
TH	Fairchild PT-19	None seen with Buzz Number. Deleted October 1949.
TJ(1)	Culver PQ-8	None seen with Buzz Number. Deleted April 1947.
TJ(2)	Convair T-29	Was TP, to TJ c. 1960.
TK	Culver PQ-14	Deleted October 1949.
TL	North American T-28A	Added in 1949.
TP	Convair T-29	Original Buzz Number for this model.
TQ	Fairchild XT-31	Proposed for Air Force version of Navy XNQ-1.
TR	Lockheed T-33A	When designated TF-80C, Buzz Number was FT, same as fighter F-80s.

North American AT-6Cs 42-43993 and 42-43956 in a classic beautiful photo taken by one of the leading aviation photographers of all time, William T. Larkins. (W. T. Larkins)

Piper PA-18 Super Cub N275T was an overall yellow trainer used by a Civil Air Patrol squadron after use by the Air Training Command. (Major E. M. Sommerich)

Judging by the curtained windows, this Beech AT-7 43-33490 seems to be assigned to a brigadier or major general. Also, a replacement left rudder is apparent, as the size and font of the 490 is different from the 333 on this fin. (W. T. Larkins)

Beech AT-11 41-9484 in another classic air-to-air shot by William T. Larkins. This aircraft seems to be from the same unit as the two AT-6Cs in the top photo. (W. T. Larkins)

Beech T-34A 53-3342. Imagine tying down a U.S. Air Force aircraft in the grass of a light plane airfield in today's climate of extreme security. (D. D. Olson)

This Cessna T-37B 56-3565 displays the extensive fluorescent orange areas on the nose, outer wings, and rear fuselage used from the late 1950s into the mid-1960s. (Norm Taylor Collection)

Northrop T-38A 59-1594 parked at the Northrop factory prior to delivery. (G. S. Williams)

This Sabreliner, North American T-39A 62-4474, was assigned to the 48th Tactical Fighter Wing at Lakenheath, England, in the early 1960s. (Bowers Collection)

The original Buzz Number on Convair T-29B 51-3816 was TP, and was changed to TJ circa 1961. This example was assigned to the 7101st Air Base Wing at Wiesbaden Air Base, Germany, and was photographed at Hahn Air Base, also in Germany. (Airman First Class Menard)

This Culver PQ-14B 44-68780 was a trainer of sorts, with an overall insignia red with yellow Buzz Number and black radio call number scheme. (W. M. Bodie)

The North American Aviation curved font shows up well on the fuse-lage markings on this Air Training Command T-28A Trojan, 49-1507 (G. S. Williams)

Someone at the Convair factory kept close track of the Buzz Numbers being painted on Convair T-29B 52-1150, as they recalled the first TP-150, 51-5150. (Bowers Collection)

A brand new Convair T-29B, 51-3816, on a factory test flight before delivery, displays the manufacturer's construction number (244) on the nose. (ASC/HO)

Lockheed T-33A-1-LO 51-6808 is displaying the original factory location and font for the T-33 Buzz Number. (Major E. M. Sommerich)

Lockheed T-33A-1-LO 50-366 is carrying a unit-applied smaller ver-sion of the Buzz Number on its nose. (Harney Collection)

Lockheed T-33A-1-LO 51-4302 displays the midfuselage location preferred by the Air Training Command. (Lieutenant Colonel Rahn)

Lockheed T-33A-1-LO 53-5050 of the 49th Tactical Fighter Wing is displaying the least-used location for this model's Buzz Number, the tail end of the fuselage. (Airman First Class Menard)

Lockheed T-33A-5-LO 55-4403 has the final factory-applied Buzz Number as displayed on the 74th Fighter Interceptor Squadron at Thule Air Base, Greenland, in May 1958. The painters seem to have ignored the T.O. requirement for bare metal borders around all standard markings when applying insignia red arctic markings. (Airman Second Class Menard)

TRAINERS: ADAPTED

Since 1943, the prefix letter T has been used on various Army Air Forces and U.S. Air Force aircraft designations to identify them as having been diverted from their designated missions to training roles.

For the most part, these were initially older models used to train combat crews in aircraft of the type they would be taking into combat, such as a TB-17 to train a complete B-17 crew during the war. However, not all aircraft with T prefixes were limited to training for that particular model. The Douglas TC-47 took advantage of its cabin space to install three student navigator stations, complete with astrodomes.

Also, during the war some adaptations became dedicated trainers. Standard bomber models were modified on the production lines and delivered as advanced trainers. Five Convair C-87s, themselves conversions of B-24 bombers, were delivered as AT-22 navigation trainers. Some 558 Martin B-26Bs and Cs were delivered as AT-23A and B pilot trainers, and 60 various North American B-25s through B-25J were delivered as AT-24s. All of these reverted to their original designations with T prefixes in 1944 and 1945. After the war, nearly 900 B-25Js were converted to TB-25K, L, M, and N.

In some cases, postwar adapted trainers have rolled out of their factories as brand new airframes with T prefixed designations, such as TF-80C, TF-102A, etc. These were single-seat designs that were extensively redesigned into dual-control two-seat aircraft, with some retaining some or all armament. The Lockheed TF-80C was so successful in its adapted role that it was put into large-scale production as a dedicated trainer, the T-33A.

Some single-seat fighters got second cockpits for tactical reasons: McDonnell F-101B/F, Lockheed F-104B/D, Republic F-105F, and Convair F-106B. The North American F-100F was a stretched two-seater without the T prefix, and was the production version of the single TF-100C.

These adapted trainers did not obtain their own Buzz Numbers but used the ones assigned to the type in the T.O. Some got modified Buzz Numbers, but this was a command decision, not from Air Force headquarters. One example is TF-XXX for a TF-51D instead of FF-XXX.

North American TB-25J-15-NC 44-28847 carries an unofficial trainer Buzz Number to possibly disguise its assignment to a senior Strategic Air Command (SAC) officer in 1955. (William J. Balogh Sr.)

Curtiss TC-46D-15-CU 44-78041 carries a TC instead of a TD Buzz Number, possibly to avoid any confusion with the T-34A, whose Buzz Number was TD. (William J. Balogh Sr.)

North American TF-51D-NT 45-11361, a target sleeve tug, carries an unofficial TF Buzz Number, replacing the normal FF symbol; it has extensive faded orange target tug colors on its tail, outer wings, and spinner. (William J. Balogh Sr.)

Boeing B-29-86-BW 44-87704 displays her TF-704 Buzz Number. It is possible that in this instance the T prefix stood for tanker and is being used unofficially to replace the standard BF Buzz Number. (USAF)

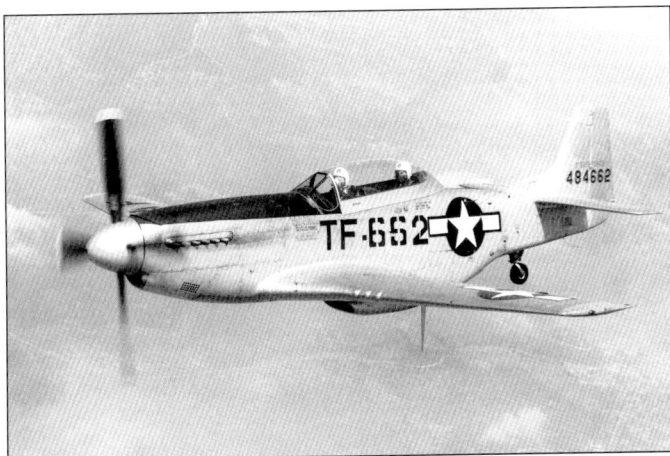

North American TF-51D-25-NT 44-84662 was one of the 10 Mustangs modified by TEMCO during the Korean War to include dual cockpits and a larger canopy. (William J. Balogh Sr.)

Lockheed TF-80C-1-LO 48-361 was the sixth example built. The new design was actually faster than the earlier F-80s and retained the fighter's Buzz Number. A total of 128 were built before the designation changed to T-33A. (USAF)

Lockheed F-80B-5-LO 45-8593 seems to be incorrectly painted, as the official Buzz Number for this model was FT, but many other Air Training Command examples also carried TF, so it may have been a command-directed marking. (Norm Taylor Collection)

Convair TF-102A-1-CO 54-1351 was the first "tub" built, and was originally assigned a trainer Buzz Number, which was eventually changed to the fighter's FC symbol. (Convair)

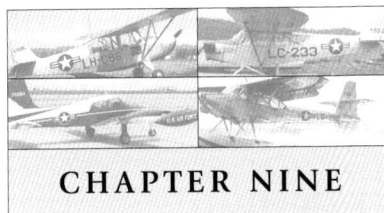

LIAISON

The letter L was added to the Army Air Forces designation system early in 1942 to distinguish the new breed of unarmed light Short Take Off and Landing (STOL) designs from the long-established O-for-observation models, which were basically single-engined light bombers, the standard since World War I. Several of the new models were basically off-the-shelf 65-horsepower civilian light planes in the Cub or "puddle jumper" class.

Several of the new designs that had already been delivered with O designations were redesignated in the new L-for-liaison series, starting with the L-1, the former O-49.

After World War II, the L category was expanded to include several new designs that had no commonality whatever with the STOL types that could operate with frontline troops. Some of these, which were basically light transports, kept their L designations, but others were redesignated. In one case, the L designation was combined with the C of a dedicated light transport to create the Cessna LC-126A and B model. However, that mixed model got neither a C nor an L Buzz Number.

As a result of the major redesignations of late 1962, some existing L models were redesignated as U-for-utility models (see sidebar) while others were put in a revived O-for-Observation category, for which no Buzz Numbers were assigned.

From 26 July 1948 to the revision of 15 July 1949, the L models were deleted from the T.O., apparently in the belief that they were all operated by the Army and therefore were of no concern to the Air Force. When this turned out to be untrue, the L models were restored to the T.O. All L models then in the inventory were given new Buzz Numbers starting with LA.

Only two of the L models that were on the original 1945 listing were still in the inventory, and they got new letters. Two postwar models that had been on the deleted list were also included in the new list, and they also received new letters. This explains why the Aeronca L-16 changed from LH to LC and North American L-17 from LJ to LD.

Not all designated L models were assigned Buzz Numbers. Some were redesignated in other categories before delivery, such as the McDonnell L-25 becoming the XV-1. The only Helio L-24 did not receive a Buzz Number, while North American L-22s became L-17Ds. The next-to-last L model, the Cessna L-27, was delivered as such but was soon redesignated in the new U-for-utility category as the U-2 (see sidebar).

Since the L planes appeared on two entirely separate lists in the T.O. and carried different Buzz Numbers on each list, the following table is divided into the same two parts.

Liaison Aircraft List No. 1
October 1945–July 1948

BUZZ NUMBER	MANUFACTURER/MODEL	REMARKS
LA	Taylorcraft L-2	None seen with Buzz Number and deleted in April 1947.
LB	Aeronca L-3	None seen with Buzz Number and deleted in April 1947.
LC	Piper L-4	Changed to LA in 1949.
LD	Stinson L-5	Changed to LB in 1949.
LE(1)	Interstate L-6	Not seen with Buzz Number and deleted in April 1947.
LE(2)	Boeing L-15	Added to list in September 1947 and not carried over to new list.
LF	Piper L-14	Not seen with Buzz Number and deleted March 1948.
LG	Convair L-13	Added September 1947 and not carried over to new list.
LH	Aeronca L-16	Added September 1947 and to LC in 1949.
LJ	North American L-17	Added September 1947 and to LD in 1949.

Liaison Aircraft List No. 2
July 1949–October 1962

BUZZ NUMBER	MANUFACTURER/MODEL	REMARKS
LA	Piper L-4	Formerly LC. Not carried in Korea.
LB	Stinson L-5	Formerly LD. Not carried in Korea. To U-19 in 1962.
LC	Aeronca L-16	Formerly LH. Not carried in Korea.
LD	North American L-17	Formerly LJ. Not carried in Korea. To U-18 in 1962.
LE	Piper L-18	Added in 1950. None seen with Buzz Number.
LF	Cessna L-19	None seen with Buzz Number. To O-1 in 1962.
LG	DeHavilland Canada L-20	Originally C-127. Added 1952. Not carried in Korea. To U-6 in 1962.
LH	Piper L-21	Not seen with Buzz Number. To U-7 in 1962.
LJ	Beech L-23	Not seen with Buzz Number. To U-8 in 1962.
LK	Aero Commander L-26	Added in 1955. Not seen with Buzz Number. Became U-4 in 1962, with later series becoming U-9 at same time.
LL	Cessna L-27	Not seen with Buzz Number. To U-3 in 1962.
LM	Helio L-28	Added 1958. Became U-10 in 1962.

Piper L-4J 45-55233 with a "first list" Buzz Number from 1949. (P. Bowers)

Stinson L-5G 45-34975 sports a "first list" Buzz Number and new U.S. AIR FORCE on fin. (G. S. Williams)

Boeing YL-15 47-432. (Bowers Collection)

CHAPTER FOURTEEN

MISCELLANEOUS COLORS

Over the years there has been a bit of confusion as to what color arctic markings were in the 1940s and 1950s, and what colors were used on target tugs, drone targets, drone directors, and other out-of-the-ordinary mission aircraft. These colors are explained in this chapter.

A drone was to be insignia red all over except the top surfaces of the wings, which were to be either white or bare metal, so the controller could tell if the drone was right side up or not. Target tugs (and sometimes drone controller aircraft) were painted overall orange (not fluorescent) on all upper and side surfaces. If orange could not be used, yellow would suffice. Both carried all standard markings for the type, including three-letter Buzz Numbers at times. The drones used white letters and numbers, and the target tugs used black or dark blue.

Over the years, there have been many descriptions of the color used on the red areas on the rear fuselages and outer wings of Air Force aircraft assigned to Arctic regions. For the record, the color used from 1945 until the late 1950s was plain old insignia red, period. Not "arctic red" or red-orange, just insignia red. These arctic markings covered the rearmost quarter of the fuselage length, to include all tail surfaces and the outer half of each wing. In practice, the wing markings started at the inboard aileron cutout and extended to the tip. At first, fabric-covered control surfaces were also painted red. This caused extra work in having to rebalance these surfaces off the aircraft, so they remained silver. One author assisted in painting many an aircraft with the red areas while stationed at Ladd Air Force Base, Alaska, in the mid-1950s. He also noted that the overall orange target tug T-33s stood out against the snow better than the red-painted aircraft and wondered why the former color was not selected for arctic markings years before.

Insignia red started to give way to a much more expensive fluorescent yellow-orange color in 1959, but within a year, fluorescent red-orange became the new color to use.

After a rash of midair collisions involving Air Force aircraft in the late 1950s, the service decided that all Air Force and Air National Guard aircraft should be painted in what was called "conspicuity" markings, using fluorescent orange color. The only aircraft exempt from these markings were Strategic Air Command bombers and Tactical Air Command and Air Defense Command fighters. These paints were very expensive, over $40 a gallon in the late 1950s! Also, their application was twice the work. First a primer coat of zinc chromate, then gloss white, then the fluorescent color, and finally a clear coat. Many writers have erroneously called these colors "day-glo," but DayGlo is actually a trademarked brand name.

These colors tended to fade quickly and were next to

North American F-86D-30-NA 51-6037 of the 37th Fighter Interceptor Squadron displays an almost textbook application of Arctic markings, as called out in the T.O. (Isham Collection)

Boeing RB-50F-50-BN 47-144 of the 55th Strategic Recon Wing has her Arctic markings painted correctly, but the painters erred in moving the tail number up on the fin and painting it in yellow instead of black. (A. L. Meyer)

Below: Boeing DB-17N-90-DL 44-83669 has been painted overall insignia orange for her role as a drone director, with the black bands designating the frequency its drones are using. (G. S. Williams via R. A. Freeman)

Lockheed T-33A-1-LO 53-5031 of the 5001st Operation Squadron, Ladd Air Force Base, Alaska, displays insignia orange top and side surfaces hastily applied in the spring of 1957. (Airman Second Class Menard)

Lockheed QF-80F 44-85462 in full drone insignia red and white livery and with extra antennas on her nose and aft section. (G. S. Williams)

impossible to touch up in a presentable manner, requiring older applications to be completely stripped before repainting. Transport aircraft had six foot bands of this color around their rear fuselages, outer wings, and noses, while smaller aircraft used three foot bands in the same locations. Because of the expense of these paints, the excess work in their application and upkeep, and short operational life while on the aircraft, the use of these colors was discontinued by the 1960s, and international orange (FS12197) became the new high-visibility color on test aircraft and arctic markings.

Some aircraft involved in test programs were painted overall gloss white to show up better during photography throughout the testing. Others got their white paint to help keep the aircraft cooler in southern climates, such as Florida and Arizona.

Many North American F-86Hs were painted overall orange at Nellis Air Force Base, Nevada, to perform duty as high-speed target tugs. (USAF)

Martin B-57E 55-4269 was built at the factory specifically to pull targets, so all upper surfaces were painted orange. (USAF)

Douglas B-26B-35-DL 41-39471 of the Fifth Tow Target Squadron from Johnson Air Base, Japan, displays her yellow tail surfaces, outer wing panels, and cowlings. (Master Sergeant M. Olmsted)

Douglas B-26B-45-DL 44-34184 of the Fourth Tow Target Squadron not only has orange tow target colors displayed, but also has full insignia red arctic markings and a yellow fin cap for unit identification. (Airman Second Class Menard)

North American F-86A-5-NA 49-1131 of the 191st Fighter Interceptor Squadron, Utah Air National Guard, displays her orange tow target colors, a green unit color on the fin, and a red flight color on the nose. (P. Paulsen)

McDonnell NF-101A-10-MC 53-2438 carries a high-speed target under her orange painted fuselage and upper surfaces. (W. M. Jefferies)

The canary yellow paint on this North American F-86A-5-NA 49-1021 of the 186th Fighter Interceptor Squadron was purchased from a local car dealership when the orange paint ran out at the All-Air National Guard Gunnery Meet at Boise, Idaho, in October 1954. (P. Paulsen)

North American F-86F-26-NH 52-5527 of the 4925th Test Group (Atomic) was painted overall red to assist in diverting any aircraft wandering into test sites where nuclear weapons were to be detonated. (S. Brown)

The overall white scheme was carried on this Douglas DB-26B-66-DL 44-34652 during airborne launching of Firebee drone targets. (Bowers Collection)

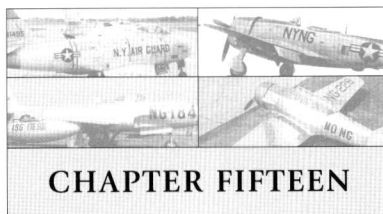

CHAPTER FIFTEEN

AIR NATIONAL GUARD

The National Guard really expanded after World War II, with many flying squadrons acquiring the lineage and honors of Army Air Forces units that had served in combat during the war. The fighter squadrons of the West and Midwest were equipped with P-51D Mustangs, while the squadrons of the East and Southeast received P-47D and N Thunderbolts. Early markings consisted of the U.S. national insignia on the top and bottom right of the wings, and either the state seal or unit insignia on the fuselage instead of the national insignia. The two-, three-, or four-letter abbreviated state name was displayed to the left of the fuselage insignia while NG was to its right. Some units placed the state name with "NG" on the center fuselage. Other units painted "NG" on the vertical fins/rudders. Eventually, the state seals gave way to the U.S. national insignia. Wing markings on the top right and bottom left consisted of "NG" followed by the last three digits of the aircraft serial number.

Some brand new fiscal year 1947 F-80Cs were delivered to a few selected National Guard units in 1948. These displayed a Buzz-Number-like NG-XXX on their noses and across the bottom of both wings and the fuselage, but no state name was displayed, for reasons unknown.

After the U.S. Air Force came into existence on 18 September 1947, it took several years for the "NG" markings to catch up and have an A inserted into them, to show Air National Guard (ANG) assignment. These "ANG" letters stayed to the right of the fuselage national insignia for the most part and on the wings with the last three digits of the serial. Tail markings were also changed to "ANG" above the radio call numbers.

These markings lasted until the late 1950s, when they were removed and replaced by new markings consisting of an abbreviated state name followed by "AIR GUARD" painted on the aircraft forward fuselages. The wing markings also changed to "AFNG" with no numbers. Some states got rather creative with their markings, painting abbreviations that looked like a foreign language. One South Dakota F-89D carried "SDAKAFNG" on its tip tanks in addition to "S DAK AIR GUARD" on each side of the nose

The 1961 Berlin Crisis saw the end to all of these large state markings permanently when many units were called up for federal service and had to have regular Air Force markings replace the state markings. The decision to retain these regular Air Force markings was to save countless man-hours of work in any future call-ups. The more subdued Air National Guard markings consisted for the most part of a round National Guard decal and a small state name painted on the vertical fins. These simplified markings carried over to the early days of camouflage in the mid-1960s.

North American T-6D 42-85258 on the 173rd Fighter Squadron, Nebraska National Guard, displays a state seal instead of a national insignia on her fuselage. (William J. Balogh Sr.)

Republic F-47D-30-RA 44-32669 of the 136th Fighter Squadron, New York National Guard, displays the early style of National Guard markings after national insignia returned to thefuselage. (Bowers Collection)

North American P-51D-25-NA 44-73578 of the 175th Fighter Squadron, South Dakota National Guard, displays the unit's original lobo insignia on her fuselage. (William J. Balogh Sr.)

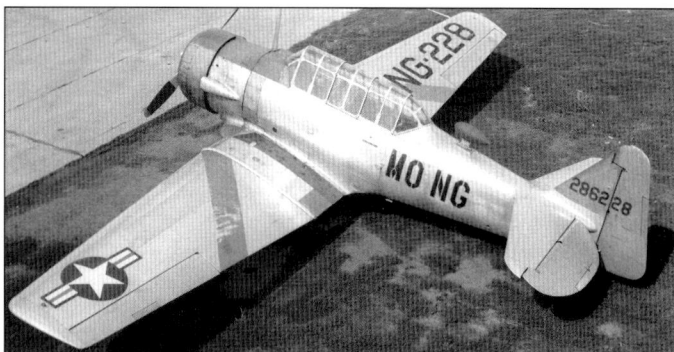

North American T-6D 42-86228 displays the National Guard wing markings and the insignia red navigation trainer markings of painted cowling, vertical tail, and diagonal wing bands. (Major E. M. Sommerich)

North American F-86H-10-NH 53-1495 of the 136th Tactical Fighter Squadron, New York Air National Guard, displays her late 1950s style Air National Guard markings, including AFNG on her wings. (Airman Second Class Menard)

Republic F-84F-25-GK 51-9388 of the 169th Tactical Fighter Squadron displays the late 1950s style Air National Guard markings at Peoria, Illinois, in May 1959. (Airman Second Class Menard)

Douglas VB-26B-66-DL 44-34610 was assigned to the National Guard Bureau as a high-speed taxi for senior officers, hence its shine job. See Chapter 11 for a view of this aircraft taken about 20 years earlier. (S. H. Miller)

Lockheed F-80C-1-LO 47-184 displays her generic factory-applied markings on her nose and California National Guard unit number on the tip tanks. (Bowers Collection)

At O'Hare Field in May 1955, Republic F-84F-15-RE 51-1563 of the 108th Fighter Bomber Squadron, Illinois Air National Guard, displays the original location for state markings on this model F-84. (Menard)

Republic F-84F-50-RE 52-6826 of the Georgia Air National Guard displays a variation on her fuselage markings location, including a period! (Bowers Collection)

Republic F-84F-40-GK 51-9507 of the 169th Tactical Fighter Squadron displays her post-1961 final Air National Guard markings, which were to remain until camouflage reappeared in the mid-1960s. (Staff Sergeant Menard)

North American F-86A-5-NA 49-1207 has had a state name removed prior to transfer to an Indiana Air National Guard unit, while displaying the wing markings in use at the time.

Northrop F-89D-20-NO 51-11364 of the 175th Fighter Interceptor Squadron, South Dakota Air National Guard, displays a very unofficial abbreviation on her tip tanks, in addition to standard markings on the nose. (Paul D. Stevens)

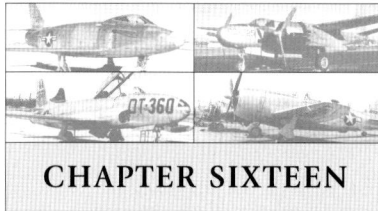

ERRORS AND ODDITIES

Since human beings were painting all of these markings, variations and mistakes had to happen. Sometimes, companies interpreted Air Force instructions in their own way (such as North American Aviation putting YF Buzz Numbers on various F-86 models), as is illustrated in this chapter. Sometimes, these instructions had to catch up to practice.

MiG-15 "47-616" in early 1954 carried an F-86A radio call number to confuse any "eavesdroppers" and a TC Buzz Number for the first names of the first two pilots, Captain Tom Collins and Major Charles Yeager. (William J. Balogh Sr.)

YaK-23 "50-599" was flown from Patterson Field with F-86E markings to help disguise its test program. (USAF)

North American RF-51D-30-NT 45-11679 was one of many camera-carrying Mustangs that displayed the unofficial RF Buzz Number. (C. Trask)

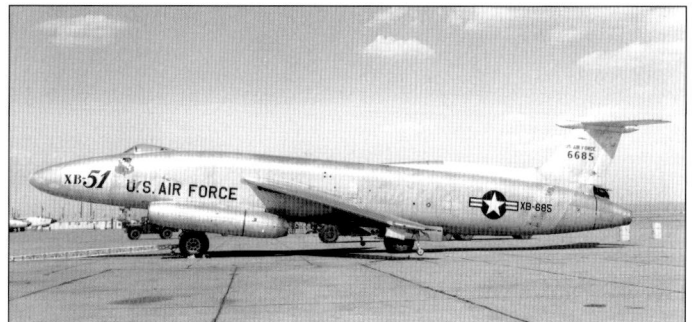

Martin XB-51 46-685 displays an unofficial Buzz Number on its fuselage in 1958. (E. Maloney)

Douglas C-47D-20-DK 43-49771 appears to be configured as a senior officer transport, so the paint crew decided to use VC instead of CE in the Buzz Number. (Bowers Collection)

North American YF-93 48-317 displays the unofficial YF Buzz Number the factory applied to many of their service test aircraft. (USAF)

North American YF-95A 50-577, with a replacement aft section fitted after the F-100 trials of the horizontal stabilizer, as indicated by the block figures displayed. (USAF)

This North American YF-95A 50-577, with a low-mounted horizontal stabilizer location, is being tested for the upcoming F-100. (USAF)

Painted overall white, North American JDF-86D-1-NA 50-462 was used to support the Navaho missile project at Cape Canaveral, Florida. (Menard Collection)

Cessna YAT-37D 62-2951, one of two prototypes for the A-37 series, displays an unofficial YT Buzz Number. This aircraft is now on display at the U.S. Air Force Museum. (USAF Museum)

These two jet aircraft, Republic EF-84D-1-REs 48-641 and 661, displaying unofficial Buzz Numbers, were involved in Project Tip Toe with EB-29A-60-BN 44-62093. (USAF)

73

After its redesignation from YAT to JAT, Cessna JAT-37D 62-2951 acquired a JT Buzz Number. (USAF Museum)

Lockheed NF-104A 56-760 displayed an unofficial Buzz Number, based on her designation. (S. H. Miller)

The "BF-387" displayed under the left wing of Republic P-47N-25-RE 44-89387 defies any explanation. Perhaps it was an Army Air Field abbreviation? (Bowers Collection)

ZDF-24B 42-54664 finished her long Air Force career with "obsolete director" (of still another Dauntless, a ZQF-24A) prefixes in 1951. We apologize for the poor quality of this image, but it is the only known view of this Buzz Number. (USAF)

North American VB-25J-32-NC 44-31324, assigned to Air Research & Development Command headquarters, is displaying an incorrect VB Buzz Number instead of BD. (R. C. Seeley)

Lockheed QF-80A-1-LO 44-85378 is ready for takeoff while displaying an unofficial Buzz Number on her nose. (USAF via R. Espostio)

North American F-51D-25-NT 45-11538 of the 12th Fighter Bomber Squadron may have had its fuselage replaced with a different one whose Buzz Number was in larger figures, hence the FF being larger than the 538. (USAF Museum)

Lockheed F-80C-10-LO 49-669 is not a painting mistake but has a borrowed aft section, which was eventually repainted. (Technical Sergeant E. Lippincott)

North American F-86D-30-NA 51-6033 of the 87th Fighter Interceptor Squadron had its Buzz Number partially obscured by unit executive officer bands. (C. Koselke)

North American F-86F-30-NA 52-4935 of the 366th Fighter Bomber wing had the five digits out of its fiscal year added incorrectly to the radio call number and an extra-wide C in the word FORCE on the fuselage. (C. Summerville)

Republic F-84E-30-RE 51-651 is also not a painting mistake, but another borrowed aft section, this time from another squadron in the wing. (E. Galbraith)

Douglas A-26B-45-DL 44-34178 of the Ninth Air Force has its Buzz Number painted incorrectly as CA-178 on its engine nacelle, where exhaust stains have obscured it into near oblivion. (William J. Balogh Sr.)

Douglas YC-124 42-65406 displays an unofficial Buzz Number of CA406 on its fin, instead of the correct radio call number of 265406. (USAF)

Stroukoff XCG-18 46-067 has its full four-digit radio call number used in its Buzz Number instead of the last three digits of 067. (Bowers Collection)

North American RF-51D-25-NT 44-84774 displays her new post-June 1948 fighter Buzz Number on her nose, while her previous F-6D FC-774 remains under the left wing. (Bowers Collection)

Republic RF-84K-17-RE 52-7266 carries a factory-applied Buzz Number on its nose and a unit-applied one on the aft fuselage. (USAF)

Douglas B-26B-66-DL 44-34725 has its Buzz Number applied twice, for unknown reasons. (Lieutenant Colonel E. Bosetti)

Lockheed T-33A-1-LO 49-1002 was transferred from one unit that used a rear fuselage location to the 50th Tactical Fighter Wing, which used the midfuselage location as on the unit's F-100s. The smaller version was removed a short time later. (Airman Second Class Menard)

Stinson L-5B 44-17157 of the Second Rescue Squadron on Okinawa not only has the U.S. AIR FORCE in letters that are much too large, but the radio call number presentation is also incorrect, as it should be 417157. (A. W. George)

Lockheed T-33A-1-LO 51-6804 carries the correct A suffix to its Buzz Number as specified by the T.O., but the painter got carried away and put it on the radio call number also. (Menard Collection)

Lockheed DTF-80C 48-360 has to be the first aircraft of this type to become a drone director. (USAF via G. Cully)

APPENDIX

The following pages from Air Force Technical Orders and Regulations were gathered over nearly 45 years in and around the USAF. They were gathered with the goal of preserving the numerous changes over these years for future historians. Over the years, mistakes such as the O prefix to the tail number meaning obsolete and the color of arctic markings being red-orange have been published and taken almost as gospel. These reproductions should correct the record once and for all. The lines on some of the documents indicate they have been rescinded but retained in the file, while other penciled notations call attention to outdated changes.

DEPARTMENT OF THE AIR FORCE
HEADQUARTERS, UNITED STATES AIR FORCE
WASHINGTON

TECHNICAL ORDER
NO. XI-1-81
APPENDIX B

11 June 1948

AIRCRAFT AND MAINTENANCE PARTS

GENERAL - MODIFICATION, CLASSIFICATION, DESIGNATION, AND REDESIGNATION OF HEAVIER-THAN-AIR AIRCRAFT

1. The purpose of this appendix is to provide a list of current Air Force inventory aircraft by present basic designator and model number together with the new type designator and prefix applicable in accordance with AF Regulation 65-60. This list does not contain complete prefix, series, and block designators and therefore is to be used for reference purposes only.

PRESENT DESIGNATOR	NEW DESIGNATOR	PRESENT DESIGNATOR	NEW DESIGNATOR	PRESENT DESIGNATOR	NEW DESIGNATOR
OA-12	A-12			C-117	C-117
OA-9	A-9	C-117		P-61	F-61
OA-10	A-10	F-2	RC-45	P-63	F-63
A-20	A-20	F-6	RF-51		
A-24	F-24			P-80	F-80
A-26	B-26	F-9	RB-17	P-81	F-81
B-17	B-17	F-10	RB-25	P-82	F-82
B-24	B-24	F-13	RB-29	P-84	F-84
B-25	B-25			CQ-3	DC-45
		F-15	RF-61		
		PG-3	G-3	PQ-14	Q-14
B-29	B-29				
B-36	B-36	CG-4	G-4	R-4	H-4
B-42	B-42	CG-10	G-10	R-5	H-5
B-43	B-43	CG-14	G-14	R-6	H-6
B-46	B-46	CG-15	G-15	R-8	H-8
B-50	B-50	L-4	L-4	R-9	H-9
C-45	C-45	L-5	L-5	R-13	H-13
C-46	C-46	L-13	L-13	AT-6	T-6
C-47	C-47				
C-53	C-53	L-16	L-16	AT-7	T-7
C-54	C-54	L-17	L-17	AT-11	T-11
C-64	C-64	P-38	F-38	*BT-13	BT-13
C-74	C-74	P-47	F-47	*PT-13	PT-13
C-82	C-82	P-51	F-51	*PT-13	T-13
C-97	C-97	P-59	F-59	PT-19	T-19
C-113	C-113				

* Since the elimination of the "B" and "P" prefixes from these aircraft would result in possible confusion by having two models of T-13 aircraft listed without identification other than serial number range, these prefixes will be retained pending withdrawal of all BT-13 aircraft from service. When this action has been accomplished, instructions will be issued to redesignate the PT-13 aircraft as T-13.

BY ORDER OF THE SECRETARY OF THE AIR FORCE:

HOYT S. VANDENBERG
Chief of Staff
United States Air Force

JOSEPH T. McNARNEY
General, United States Air Force
Commanding General
Air Materiel Command

Prepared by Maintenance Technical Section,
Maintenance Div, Hq, AMC.

NOTICE: Reproduction of the information or illustrations contained in this publication is not permitted without specific approval of the issuing service.

WF (A)--O--6-11-48--5700

AIR FORCE REGULATION)
NO. 65-60

*AFR 65-60
1-3

DEPARTMENT OF THE AIR FORCE
WASHINGTON, 11 JUNE 1948

SUPPLY AND MAINTENANCE

Modification, Classification, Designation, and Redesignation of Heavier-than-air Aircraft

SECTION I - GENERAL

	Paragraph
Purpose	1
Definitions	2

SECTION II - TERMINOLOGY FOR HEAVIER-THAN-AIR AIRCRAFT

	Paragraph
Designator Assignment	3
Prefix Symbols	4
Classification Symbols	5
Component Assignment Identification	6
Complete Aircraft Designator	7
Reporting	8

SECTION III - MODIFICATION AND REDESIGNATION RESPONSIBILITIES AND POLICIES

	Paragraph
General	9
Authorization of Certain Modifications by Air Materiel Command	10
Authorization of Certain Modifications by Air Proving Ground	11
Air Materiel Command	12
Air Training Command	13
Headquarters USAF	14
Modification and Redesignation Policy	15
Statistical Grouping	16
TO 01-1-81	17

SECTION I - GENERAL

1. **Purpose.** This Regulation authorizes the symbols to be used in identifying all Air Force heavier-than-air aircraft and defines the policies and responsibilities relative to aircraft modification, classification, designation, and redesignation.

2. **Definitions:**

a. "Type" as applied to aircraft designates the original design purpose of an aircraft, i.e., bombardment, fighter, cargo, etc.

b. "Model" as applied to aircraft designates those aircraft of a given type which are alike in general configuration, construction, equipment, and performance.

c. "Series" as applied to aircraft designates those aircraft of a given type and model having, for all practical purposes, interchangeable parts and identical tactical usefulness.

d. "Modification" of aircraft is defined as any change in structure, arrangement, or additions or deletions to that equipment incorporated in the aircraft.

SECTION II - TERMINOLOGY FOR HEAVIER-THAN-AIR AIRCRAFT

3. **Designator Assignment.** Aircraft will be assigned a basic type designator in accordance with the function for which they are basically designed. When a type of aircraft is modified to

*This pamphlet supersedes AFR 65-60, 17 June 1947 and AFR 65-15, 27 March 1947; and rescinds AFL 65-124, 18 December 1945.

BROOKLEY FLD, ALA. 6-24-48-700

8-7370, AF

78

AFR 65-6(
4

longer applicable. Authorization for the use of these symbols will be obtained in accordance with section III of this Regulation. Modification of aircraft, except as noted herein, is not authorized without appropriate redesignation. As an example of this redesignation, a B-50A-10-BO aircraft modified as a reconnaissance aircraft will be redesignated an RB-50A-10-BO. An aircraft so redesignated will retain this prefix until such time as those features which provided its reconnaissance characteristics are removed and it is restored to its original basic condition or re-modified for an entirely different function. Only in exceptional cases will more than one prefix symbol be used to designate an aircraft. Such an exception could occur, for example, if an RF-80 is modified for reconnaissance training. It would then be redesignated as a TRF-80. However, if it is modified for normal training purposes, it should become a TF-80. If more than one prefix symbol is used, the first symbol from the left will be considered the primary prefix symbol and the next one the secondary prefix symbol.

a. Prefix "B." The prefix symbol "B" will be used to designate aircraft modified to function as bomber type aircraft, i.e., the inclusion of a bombardier nose in fighter type aircraft. The addition of external bomb, torpedo, or depth-charge carrying devices and dive or skip bombing sighting equipment on any basic type aircraft does not constitute sufficient cause for the redesignation of that aircraft as "B" type.

b. Prefix "C." The prefix symbol "C" will be used to designate aircraft specifically modified for cargo use. Basic type aircraft utilized for cargo purposes without modification will not be redesignated with the prefix "C."

c. Prefix "D." The prefix symbol "D" will be used to designate those aircraft which are modified to function as director aircraft in conjunction with remotely controlled aircraft or guided missiles. (See AFR 58-5.)

d. Prefix "F." The prefix symbol "F" will be used to designate basic aircraft modified for fighter operations. The addition of rocket launchers on liaison or rotary wing aircraft does not constitute sufficient cause for redesignation as "F" type aircraft.

e. Prefix "G." The prefix symbol "G" will be used to designate those powered aircraft after modifications removing all means of self-contained thrust have been completed.

f. Prefix "L." The prefix symbol "L" will be used to designate aircraft modified for liaison missions. The use of this prefix will be extremely limited.

g. Prefix "M." The prefix symbol "M" will be used to designate aircraft modified for use as missiles. (See AFR 58-5.)

h. Prefix "Q." The prefix symbol "Q" will be used to designate basic aircraft modified through the inclusion of special electronic equipment for use as targets or drones.

i. Prefix "R." The prefix symbol "R" will be used to designate those basic aircraft which have been so modified as to make them suitable for reconnaissance missions, i.e., weather reconnaissance, photo reconnaissance, etc.

j. Prefix "S." The prefix symbol "S" will be used to designate basic aircraft modified through the inclusion of special search electronic equipment, airborne life boats, life rafts, or extensive life saving equipment, etc. This symbol will not be used to redesignate those aircraft utilized for air evacuation of litter patients.

k. Prefix "T." The prefix symbol "T" will be used to designate those aircraft which have had equipment removed to make them more suitable for training purposes. This symbol wil also be used to designate those aircraft modified through the inclusion of special training equipment, i.e., navigator trainers, engineer trainers, etc. Aircraft used for training purposes for which authorization to remove equipment has not been granted, will not carry the prefix "T." "T" prefixed aircraft will not be considered suitable for return to combat status; therefore, the "T" prefix normally will not be authorized to combat potential aircraft.

l. Prefix "V." The prefix symbol "V" will be used to designate those aircraft whic are modified as staff administrative transports. This will include modified cargo types.

3 8-7370, AF

AFR 65-60
5-6

5. Classification Symbols. Aircraft may have any one of the following classification symbols applied where applicable.

a. Classification "E." The classification symbol "E" (Exempt) will be used to designate those aircraft on special tests or experimental projects by authorized activities and for aircraft on bailment contract (Work contracted for by a nonmilitary agency using AF-owned aircraft). Aircraft utilized in special tests, experimental projects, or bailment contracts that have not received modifications and where the interchangeability of the aircraft with like type, model, series, and block aircraft has not been affected, will not be classified with the symbol "E." At the termination of tests, etc., "E" classified aircraft will either be returned to their original condition and designation or, if certain modifications become a permanent part of the aircraft, an appropriate redesignation of prefix, series, or block, other than "E," will be made. The "E" classification is not applicable to "X" classified aircraft.

b. Classification "X." The classification symbol "X" will be used to designate experimental aircraft and indicates that the item being developed has not progressed to the stage where engineering tests indicate that the item is sufficiently satisfactory to warrant service tests.

c. Classification "Y." The classification symbol "Y" will be used to designate those aircraft which have the required military characteristics and are of a quantity produced to develop the potentialities of the model. This classification indicates the item has been developed beyond the experimental stage, but is not ready for classification as an adopted item.

d. Classification "Z." The classification symbol "Z" will be used to designate aircraft which are considered by the Chief of Staff, USAF, to be obsolete and of and for which no further procurement will be made. Obsolete aircraft are those aircraft that are declared unsuitable for their original military purposes or for training purposes.

The assignment of a classification symbol to an aircraft will replace any prefix symbol which the aircraft currently possesses, except where the aircraft concerned retains those characteristics and/or equipment which previously classified it under the type indicated by the prefix. In such exceptional cases, the assignment of the classification symbol will be in addition to the prefix symbol. For example, if an RB-17 is placed on bailment contract and is modified, but still retains its reconnaissance features, it would be reclassified as an ERB-17. However, if its reconnaissance equipment is removed, it would become an EB-17. On the other hand if this aircraft is completely superseded by more modern aircraft, it would become a ZRB-17. If, while still in service, the reconnaissance equipment is removed, it then becomes a ZB-17. In no instance will the aircraft classification, prefix, and type designator exceed three symbols. In the event a classification symbol is assigned an aircraft already designated with two prefixes, only the most important prefix will be retained.

6. Component Assignment Identification:

a. To facilitate proper auditing and cost accounting, it is necessary to indicate to which component of the military establishment an aircraft is assigned. The components and their approved designation symbols are as follows:

COMPONENT	SYMBOL
U. S. Air Force	A
U. S. Army	G
Air Attache	M
National Guard	N
Air Reserve	R
R.O.T.C.	T

4 8-7370, AF

AFR 65-60
6-10

b. The appropriate symbol will be used as a suffix immediately following the aircraft serial number. This symbol will be shown on the fuselage of the aircraft after the aircraft serial number placed on the left-hand side of the fuselage in the vicinity of the pilot's position. Assignment symbols will also be reflected on all forms, charts, and other listings pertaining to the aircraft. As an example of this provision, USAF B-29, serial number 45-61717 will have an "A" added to its serial number thus becoming 45-61717A. Similarly, USA L-4J, serial number 45-4822, will become 45-4822G.

7. Complete Aircraft Designator. For reference purposes a complete aircraft designator and serial number is shown below:

Class. or Aux. Prefix	Prefix	Basic Type Designator		Model	Series		Block		Manufacturer	Serial Number	Component Assignment
E	R	B	-	50	A	-	10	-	BO	45-61717	A

8. Reporting. For reporting purposes, the complete type, model, and series designation, including the prefix or classification symbol(s) will be used by service activities in all statistical reports to indicate the current usage and assignment of the aircraft. The addition or change of a prefix or classification will be reported on AF Form 110B as a redesignation as provided in AFR 15-110.

SECTION III - MODIFICATION AND REDESIGNATION RESPONSIBILITIES AND POLICIES

9. General. Commanders will maintain in combat readiness those aircraft assigned to their respective commands necessary to perform combat missions assigned to them under existing directives. All commands and activities desiring modification or redesignation for permanently assigned aircraft will submit requests to the Commanding General, Air Materiel Command. The request will indicate the affected aircraft by complete designators, including block and serial number, its intended usage, and a brief but concise description of the modifications or changes desired for that usage. In order to minimize the problem of maintenance, supply, and distribution and to effect the maximum economy it is essential that modifications of aircraft be held to an absolute minimum. No modification of aircraft, except as noted in subsequent paragraphs of this Regulation, will be performed by any command or activity without the final approval of Headquarters USAF.

10. Authorization of Certain Modifications by Air Materiel Command. The Commanding General, Air Materiel Command, may authorize modification of aircraft in the following cases:

a. Technical changes relating purely to safety, to the mechanical operation of the aircraft, or to the maintenance and servicing of the aircraft but not affecting its military characteristics. Technical changes so approved will be authorized normally by appropriate Technical Orders.

b. Emergency modifications of a minor nature such as stripping or changes in interior arrangements which can be accomplished within the activity to which the aircraft is assigned without expenditure of Federal funds for materials or equipment, provided that removal or reinstallation of equipment to return the aircraft to its designated condition can be accomplished by the normal maintenance crews within a single 24-hour period. Request for emergency modifications of this nature will be submitted in accordance with paragraph 9. All aircraft will be restored to their original condition at the end of the emergency. Air Materiel Command will be notified by wire when the restoration is complete.

5 8-7370, AF

AFR 65-60
10-15

c. Modifications which may be required in the execution of authorized service tests under the provisions of AFR 65-102.

11. Authorization of Certain Modifications by Air Proving Ground. The Commanding General, Air Proving Ground, may authorize modifications necessary in the execution of special tests as prescribed in AFR 20-14, provided the modifications are of a temporary nature and complete restoration of the aircraft is made upon the completion of all tests.

12. Air Materiel Command. The Commanding General, Air Materiel Command, will be responsible for:

a. Assuring that all modifications of like character, i.e., photo reconnaissance, air-sea rescue, training, drone, etc., are standardized wherever possible. This will include the assembly and maintaining of standard modification data for distribution to affected activities.

b. Submission to Headquarters USAF with recommendations for approval or disapproval those modification and redesignation requests received in accordance with paragraph 9. All modification and redesignation requests forwarded to Headquarters USAF will contain a brief but concise statement as to availability of the required supplies in AF stock and the estimated labor (civilian and military) and material cost.

c. Assignment of prefix and classification symbols, model numbers, series letters, block designators, and manufacturer's code symbols to all aircraft produced in individual factories or modified in production or service activities.

d. Preparation, publication, distribution, and revision as required of Technical Orders to direct the classification and redesignation of aircraft in service.

e. Preparation, publication, distribution, and revision as required of the changes made in production and service modified aircraft. This datum will contain full explanatory information to identify each type, model, series, and block change to aircraft excluding "V" prefixed and "E," "X," "Y," and "Z" classified aircraft. Where practicable, this procedure will be made retroactive to cover current first-line aircraft.

13. Air Training Command. The Commanding General, Air Training Command, will be responsible for initiating lists of strippable items or modifications required to convert combat aircraft to training aircraft ("T" prefixed). These lists will be forwarded to Headquarters USAF through the Commanding General, Air Materiel Command, and will be used as standard "T" modification data. Installation provisions, such as mounts, brackets, and other attaching parts for equipment designated for removal from "T" prefixed aircraft will not be included in these lists and will not be removed when any aircraft is stripped or modified for training purposes.

14. Headquarters USAF. Headquarters USAF will approve bulk reclassification of aircraft (including line of aircraft) by type, model, series, and block number in accordance with the latest modernization policies and tactical considerations.

15. Modification and Redesignation Policy:

a. "Z" classified aircraft may be stripped of miscellaneous armament, photographic, communication, oxygen, and navigational equipment not required in the specific mission assignment of the aircraft. The removal of this equipment is subject only to the approval of the commanding general of the command under which the aircraft is assigned. This authority does not include the removal of any installation provisions, such as mounts, brackets, or other attaching parts for equipment or the installation of equipment other than that authorized for installation in the aircraft at the time of its classification as "Z" aircraft. Authority to install additional equipment in "Z" aircraft will be obtained in accordance with paragraph 9.

b. "T" designated and "T" prefixed aircraft may be stripped of miscellaneous armament, photographic, communication, oxygen, and navigational equipment not required in the specific mission assignment of the aircraft. Removal of this equipment is subject only to the approval of the commanding general of the command to which the aircraft is assigned. This authority does not include the removal of any installation provisions, such as mounts, brackets,

6 8-7370, AF

14. _Air Training Command._ The Commanding General, Air Training Command, will be responsible for initiating lists of strippable items or modifications required to convert combat aircraft to training aircraft ("T" prefixed). These lists will be forwarded to Headquarters USAF through the Commanding General, Air Materiel Command, and will be used as standard "T" modification data. Installation provisions, such as mounts, brackets, and other attaching parts for equipment designated for removal from "T" prefixed aircraft will not be included in these lists and will not be removed when any aircraft is stripped or modified for training purposes.

15. _Headquarters USAF._ Headquarters USAF will approve bulk reclassification of aircraft (including line of aircraft) by type, model, series, and block number in accordance with the latest modernization policies and tactical considerations.

16. _Modification and Redesignation Policy:_

a. "Z" classified aircraft may be stripped of miscellaneous armament, photographic, communication, oxygen, and navigational equipment not required in the specific mission assignment of the aircraft. The removal of this equipment is subject only to the approval of the commanding general of the command under which the aircraft is assigned. This authority does not include the removal of any installation provisions, such as mounts, brackets, or other attaching parts for equipment or the installation of equipment other than that authorized for installation in the aircraft at the time of its classification as "Z" aircraft. Authority to install additional equipment in "Z" aircraft will be obtained in accordance with paragraph 9.

b. "T" designated and "T" prefixed aircraft may be stripped of miscellaneous armament, photographic, communication, oxygen, and navigational equipment not required in the specific mission assignment of the aircraft. Removal of this equipment is subject only to the approval of the commanding general of the command, or in the case of the Air National Guard, the appropriate Adjutant General of the State to which the aircraft is assigned. This authority does not include the removal of any installation provisions, such as mounts, brackets, or other attaching parts for equipment or the installation of equipment other than that authorized for installation by applicable directives for the specific "T" designated or "T" prefixed aircraft. Authority to install additional equipment in "T" designated and "T" prefixed aircraft will be obtained in accordance with paragraph 9 or 10d whichever is applicable.

c. Modification undertaken by the Air Materiel Command will, in general, be only that work beyond the capabilities of the operating activity possessing the aircraft. If necessary, in the interest of expediting completion of projects, the Air Materiel Command may make arrangements with other commands for assistance. All such work thus accomplished will be under the general supervision of and in accordance with technical instructions furnished by the Air Materiel Command. Modifications undertaken by commands other than the Air Materiel Command will be in accordance with Air Materiel Command approved drawings or technical instructions.

d. Equipment removed from aircraft in accordance with paragraphs 10b and b above, will be stored by the activity to which the aircraft is assigned and reinstalled prior to the transfer of the aircraft. Equipment removed in accordance with a above will be returned to Air Force supply.

e. Aircraft modified in accordance with paragraphs 10a and b will not require redesignation.

f. Aircraft modified in accordance with paragraphs 10c and 11, when the interchangeability of the aircraft with like type, model and series has been affected, will be redesignated as "E" or "X" aircraft (paragraph 5b) if such modification is permanent.

g. Staff administrative aircraft modifications ("V" prefixed) will be governed by the following:

(1) No aircraft will be modified as a staff administrative transport except basic cargo ("C") and trainer ("T") types.

(2) Normally only twin engine aircraft will be modified as staff administrative transports. However, 4-engine aircraft may be utilized subject to availability in the Air Force inventory.

9-6733, AF

17. _Statistical Grouping._ For purposes of statistical grouping of types of aircraft the following principles will be followed:

a. All aircraft with basic type designator only will always be classed under the basic type, e.g., B-50A-10: Bomber Type.

b. All aircraft with the basic type designator prefixed by another designator authorized as a prefix symbol excluding the prefixes "D," "M," and "V" ("B," "C," "F," "G," "L," "Q," "R," "S," and "T"), will always be classed under the type indicated by the primary prefix, e.g., ERB-50A-10: Reconnaissance Type.

18. _TO 01-1-81._ Appropriate implementing instructions for this Regulation are contained in Technical Order 01-1-81.

BY ORDER OF THE SECRETARY OF THE AIR FORCE:

HOYT S. VANDENBERG
Chief of Staff, United States Air Force

OFFICIAL:

L. L. JUDGE
Colonel, USAF
Air Adjutant General

DISTRIBUTION:
D; G

APPENDIX

CHANGE

AFR 65-60A
4-9

AIR FORCE REGULATION)
NO. 65-60A)

DEPARTMENT OF THE AIR FORCE
WASHINGTON, 30 AUGUST 1950

SUPPLY AND MAINTENANCE

Modification, Classification, Designation, and Redesignation of Heavier-than-air Aircraft

AFR 65-60, 9 May 1949, is changed as follows:

4. *Prefix Symbols.* The symbols listed below will be used as prefix symbols to indicate the current usage of an aircraft when it is so modified that its originally intended usage is no longer applicable. Authorization for the use of these symbols will be obtained in accordance with section III of this Regulation. Modification of aircraft, except as noted herein, is not authorized without appropriate redesignation. As an example of this redesignation, a B-50A-10-BO aircraft modified as a reconnaissance aircraft will be redesignated an RB-50A-10-BO. An aircraft so redesignated will retain this prefix until such time as those features which provided its reconnaissance characteristics are removed and it is restored to its original basic condition or remodified for an entirely different function. Only in exceptional cases will more than one prefix symbol be used to designate an aircraft. Such an exception could occur, for example, if an RF-80 is modified for reconnaissance training. It would then be redesignated as a TRF-80. However, if it is modified for normal training purposes, it should become a TF-80. If more than one prefix symbol is used, the first symbol from the left will be considered the primary prefix symbol and the next one the secondary prefix symbol.

f. *Prefix "K."* The prefix symbol "K" will be used to designate all aircraft modified as "inflight" refueling tankers.

j. *Prefix "R."* The prefix symbol "R" will be used to designate those basic aircraft which have been so modified as to make them suitable for photo and/or electronics reconnaissance missions.

l. *Prefix "T."* The prefix symbol "T" will be used to designate those aircraft which have had equipment removed to make them suitable for training purposes. This symbol will be used to designate those aircraft modified through the inclusion of special training equipment; i.e., navigator trainers, engineer trainers, etc. Aircraft used for training purposes for which authorization to remove equipment has not been granted, will not carry the prefix "T." "T" prefixed aircraft will not be considered suitable for return to combat status; therefore, the "T" prefix will not be authorized to combat potential aircraft.

n. *Prefix "W."* The prefix symbol "W" will be used to designate those basic aircraft which have been so modified as to make them suitable for weather reconnaissance missions.

9. *General.*

a. Commanders will maintain in readiness those aircraft assigned to their respective commands necessary to perform the missions assigned to them under existing directives. Normally, no tactical or transport types will be modified into training, administrative, or other types. All commands and activities desiring modification or redesignation for permanently assigned aircraft will submit requests to Headquarters USAF, Deputy Chief of Staff, Operations, Washington 25, D. C., except as noted in subsequent paragraphs of this Regulation. The request will indicate the affected aircraft by complete

51-1187, AF

AFR 65-60
3-4

perform a function other than its basically designed function, the basic type designator will be prefixed by the appropriate auxiliary symbol. Aircraft will not be redesignated merely on the basis of current usage.

a. *Type.* The basic type designation will consist of one letter as follows:

A	Amphibious
*B	Bomber
*C	Cargo
*F	Fighter
*G	Glider
H	Rotary Wing (Helicopter)
*L	Liaison
*Q	Target Aircraft and Drones
*R	Reconnaissance
S	Search and Rescue
*T	Trainer
**X	Special Research or Experimental

NOTE: *To be used as prefix symbols as required.
**To be used as a classification symbol as required.

b. *Model.* A particular model of a given type will be designated by a number or numbers separated from the preceding type letter or letters by a dash, such as B-50.

c. *Series.* Following the model number there will always be a series letter, such as B-50A. (This provision is not retroactive.) The letters "O" and "I" will not be used. The series letters of a model will be changed when:

(1) A change is made in the engine which materially affects the engine performance rating or seriously affects the interchangeability in the aircraft.

(2) A change is made in propellers which affects interchangeability (Curtiss instead of Hamilton Standard) or flying characteristics of an aircraft (13'6" propellers instead of 12'6" propellers).

(3) A major change is made in primary installed armament (Addition of chin turret, addition of side guns, installation of 20mm guns instead of .50 caliber, etc.).

(4) A major change is made in structure and/or equipment installation affecting interchangeability.

d. *Block Number.* Following the type, model, and series designations, there will always be a block designation number consisting of one, two, or three digits to designate production releases with respect to changes affecting safety, utility, and interchangeability. (This provision is not retroactive.) The block designation (either one, two, or three digits) will denote a group of aircraft, the parts and modifications of which are identical from a maintenance and servicing standpoint and the uses of which are identical from a tactical standpoint. The block number will be separated from the rest of the designation by a dash, such as B-50A-10 and will be assigned to production aircraft as one (1), five (5), and multiples of five (5). Intermediate block numbers will be reserved for assignment by Air Materiel Command, as considered necessary. For example, a B-50A-10 will, at the first service modification, become a B-50A-11.

e. *Manufacturer's Code Symbols.* Following the block designation, there will be a two-letter code symbol identifying the manufacturer of the individual aircraft as specified in AF Bulletin 52 ("Aircraft Manufacturers' Code Symbols," published by Air Materiel Command). The manufacturer's symbols will be separated from the block designation by a dash. Example of a complete aircraft designation: B-50A-10-BO.

4. *Prefix Symbols.* The symbols listed below will be used as prefix symbols to indicate the current usage of an aircraft when it is so modified that its originally intended usage is no

2

8-7370, AF

AFR 65-60
4

longer applicable. Authorization for the use of these symbols will be obtained in accordance with section III of this Regulation. Modification of aircraft, except as noted herein, is not authorized without appropriate redesignation. As an example of this redesignation, a B-50A-10-BO aircraft modified as a reconnaissance aircraft will be redesignated an RB-50A-10-BO. An aircraft so redesignated will retain this prefix until such time as those features which provided its reconnaissance characteristics are removed and it is restored to its original basic condition or remodified for an entirely different function. Only in exceptional cases will more than one prefix symbol be used to designate an aircraft. Such an exception could occur, for example, if an RF-80 is modified for reconnaissance training. It would then be redesignated as a TRF-80. However, if it is modified for normal training purposes, it should become a TF-80. If more than one prefix symbol is used, the first symbol from the left will be considered the primary prefix symbol and the next one the secondary prefix symbol.

a. *Prefix "B."* The prefix symbol "B" will be used to designate aircraft modified to function as bomber type aircraft, i.e., the inclusion of a bombardier nose in fighter type aircraft. The addition of external bomb, torpedo, or depth-charge carrying devices and dive or skip bombing sighting equipment on any basic type aircraft does not constitute sufficient cause for the redesignation of that aircraft as "B" type.

b. *Prefix "C."* The prefix symbol "C" will be used to designate aircraft specifically modified for cargo use. Basic type aircraft utilized for cargo purposes without modification will not be redesignated with the prefix "C."

c. *Prefix "D."* The prefix symbol "D" will be used to designate those aircraft which are modified to function as director aircraft in conjunction with remotely controlled aircraft or guided missiles. (See AFR 58-5.)

d. *Prefix "F."* The prefix symbol "F" will be used to designate basic aircraft modified for fighter operations. The addition of rocket launchers on liaison or rotary wing aircraft does not constitute sufficient cause for redesignation as "F" type aircraft.

e. *Prefix "G."* The prefix symbol "G" will be used to designate those powered aircraft after modifications removing all means of self-contained thrust have been completed.

f. *Prefix "L."* The prefix symbol "L" will be used to designate aircraft modified for liaison missions. The use of this prefix will be extremely limited.

g. *Prefix "M."* The prefix symbol "M" will be used to designate aircraft modified for use as missiles. (See AFR 58-5.)

h. *Prefix "Q."* The prefix symbol "Q" will be used to designate basic aircraft modified through the inclusion of special electronic equipment for use as targets or drones.

i. *Prefix "R."* The prefix symbol "R" will be used to designate those basic aircraft which have been so modified as to make them suitable for reconnaissance missions, i.e., weather reconnaissance, photo reconnaissance, etc.

j. *Prefix "S."* The prefix symbol "S" will be used to designate basic aircraft modified through the inclusion of special search electronic equipment, airborne life boats, life rafts, or extensive life saving equipment, etc. This symbol will not be used to redesignate those aircraft utilized for air evacuation of litter patients.

k. *Prefix "T."* The prefix symbol "T" will be used to designate those aircraft which have had equipment removed to make them more suitable for training purposes. This symbol will also be used to designate those aircraft modified through the inclusion of special training equipment, i.e., navigator trainers, engineer trainers, etc. Aircraft used for training purposes for which authorization to remove equipment has not been granted, will not carry the prefix "T." "T" prefixed aircraft will not be considered suitable for return to combat status; therefore, the "T" prefix normally will not be authorized to combat potential aircraft.

l. *Prefix "V."* The prefix symbol "V" will be used to designate those aircraft which are modified as staff administrative transports. This will include modified cargo types.

3

8-7370, AF

AFR 65-60
5-6

5. Classification Symbols. Aircraft may have any one of the following classification symbols applied where applicable.

a. Classification "E." The classification symbol "E" (Exempt) will be used to designate those aircraft on special tests or experimental projects by authorized activities and for aircraft on bailment contract (Work contracted for by a nonmilitary agency using AF-owned aircraft). Aircraft utilized in special tests, experimental projects, or bailment contracts that have not received modifications and where the interchangeability of the aircraft with like type, model, series, and block aircraft has not been affected, will not be classified with the symbol "E." At the termination of tests, etc., "E" classified aircraft will either be returned to their original condition and designation or, if certain modifications become a permanent part of the aircraft, an appropriate redesignation of prefix, series, or block,•other than "E," will be made. The "E" classification is not applicable to "X" classified aircraft.

b. Classification "X." The classification symbol "X" will be used to designate experimental aircraft and indicates that the item being developed has not progressed to the stage where engineering tests indicate that the item is sufficiently satisfactory to warrant service tests.

c. Classification "Y." The classification symbol "Y" will be used to designate those aircraft which have the required military characteristics and are of a quantity produced to develop the potentialities of the model. This classification indicates the item has been developed beyond the experimental stage, but is not ready for classification as an adopted item.

d. Classification "Z." The classification symbol "Z" will be used to designate aircraft which are considered by the Chief of Staff, USAF. to be obsolete and of and for which no further procurement will be made. Obsolete aircraft are those aircraft that are declared unsuitable for their original military purposes or for training purposes.

The assignment of a classification symbol to an aircraft will replace any prefix symbol which the aircraft currently possesses, except where the aircraft concerned retains those characteristics and/or equipment which previously classified it under the type indicated by the prefix. In such exceptional cases, the assignment of the classification symbol will be in addition to the prefix symbol. For example, if an RB-17 is placed on bailment contract an ERB-17. However, if its retains its reconnaissance features, it would be reclassified as an EB-17. On the other hand if this aircraft is completely superseded by more modern aircraft, it would become a ZRB-17. If, while still in service, the reconnaissance equipment is removed, it then becomes a ZB-17. In no instance will the aircraft classification, prefix, and type designator exceed three symbols. In the event a classification symbol is assigned an aircraft already designated with two prefixes, only the most important prefix will be retained.

6. Component Assignment Identification:

a. To facilitate proper auditing and cost accounting, it is necessary to indicate to which component of the military establishment an aircraft is assigned. The components and their approved designation symbols are as follows:

COMPONENT	SYMBOL
U. S. Air Force	A
U. S. Army	G
Air Attache	M
National Guard	N
Air Reserve	R
R.O.T.C.	T

AFR 65-60
6-10

b. The appropriate symbol will be used as a suffix immediately following the aircraft serial number. This symbol will be shown on the fuselage of the aircraft after the aircraft serial number placed on the left-hand side of the fuselage in the vicinity of the pilot's position. Assignment symbols will also be reflected on all forms, charts, and other listings pertaining to the aircraft. As an example of this provision, USAF B-29, serial number 45-61717A. Similarly, USA L-4J, serial number "A" added to its serial number thus becoming 45-61717A. Similarly, USA L-4J, serial number 45-4822, will become 45-4822G.

7. Complete Aircraft Designator. For reference purposes a complete aircraft designator and serial number is shown below:

Class. or Aux. Prefix	Prefix	Basic Type Designator	Model	Series	Block	Manufacturer	Serial Number	Component Assignment
E	R	B	-50	A	-10	-BO	45-61717	A

8. Reporting. For reporting purposes, the complete type, model, and series designation, including the prefix or classification symbol(s) will be used by service activities in all statistical reports to indicate the current usage and assignment of the aircraft. The addition or change of a prefix or classification will be reported on AF Form 110B as a redesignation as provided in AFR 15-110.

SECTION III - MODIFICATION AND REDESIGNATION RESPONSIBILITIES AND POLICIES

9. General. Commanders will maintain in combat readiness those aircraft assigned to their respective commands necessary to perform combat missions assigned to them under existing directives. All commands and activities desiring modification or redesignation for permanently assigned aircraft will submit requests to the Commanding General, Air Materiel Command. The request will indicate the affected aircraft by complete designators, including block and serial number, its intended usage, and a brief but concise description of the modifications or changes desired for that usage. In order to minimize the problem of maintenance, supply, and distribution and to effect the maximum economy it is essential that modifications of aircraft be held to an absolute minimum. No modification of aircraft, except as noted in subsequent paragraphs of this Regulation, will be performed by any command or activity without the final approval of Headquarters USAF.

10. Authorization of Certain Modifications by Air Materiel Command. The Commanding General, Air Materiel Command, may authorize modification of aircraft in the following cases:

a. Technical changes relating purely to safety, to the mechanical operation of the aircraft, or to the maintenance and servicing of the aircraft but not affecting its military characteristics. Technical changes so approved will be authorized normally by appropriate Technical Orders.

b. Emergency modifications of a minor nature such as stripping or changes in interior arrangements which can be accomplished within the activity to which the aircraft is assigned without expenditure of Federal funds for materials or equipment, provided that removal or reinstallation of equipment to return the aircraft to its designated condition can be accomplished by the normal maintenance crews within a single 24-hour period. Request for emergency modifications of this nature will be submitted in accordance with paragraph 9. All aircraft will be restored to their original condition at the end of the emergency. Air Materiel Command will be notified by wire when the restoration is complete.

5

8-7370, AF

APPENDIX

AFR 65-60
10-15

c. Modifications which may be required in the execution of authorized service tests under the provisions of AFR 65-102.

11. **Authorization of Certain Modifications by Air Proving Ground.** The Commanding General, Air Proving Ground, may authorize modifications necessary in the execution of special tests as prescribed in AFR 20-14, provided the modifications are of a temporary nature and complete restoration of the aircraft is made upon the completion of all tests.

12. **Air Materiel Command.** The Commanding General, Air Materiel Command, will be responsible for:

a. Assuring that all modifications of like character, i.e., photo reconnaissance, air-sea rescue, training, drone, etc., are standardized wherever possible. This will include the assembly and maintaining of standard modification data for distribution to affected activities.

b. Submission to Headquarters USAF with recommendations for approval or disapproval those modification and redesignation requests received in accordance with paragraph 9. All modification and redesignation requests forwarded to Headquarters USAF will contain a brief but concise statement as to availability of the required supplies in AF stock and the estimated labor (civilian and military) and material cost.

c. Assignment of prefix and classification symbols, model numbers, series letters, block designators, and manufacturer's code symbols to all aircraft produced in individual factories or modified in production or service activities.

d. Preparation, publication, distribution, and revision as required of Technical Orders to direct the classification and redesignation of aircraft in service.

e. Preparation, publication, distribution, and revision as required of the changes made in production and service modified aircraft. This datum will contain full explanatory information to identify each type, model, series, and block change to aircraft excluding "V" prefixed and "E," "X," "Y," and "Z" classified aircraft. Where practicable, this procedure will be made retroactive to cover current first-line aircraft.

13. **Air Training Command.** The Commanding General, Air Training Command, will be responsible for initiating lists of strippable items or modifications required to convert combat aircraft to training aircraft ("T" prefixed). These lists will be forwarded to Headquarters USAF through the Commanding General, Air Materiel Command, and will be used as standard "T" modification data. Installation provisions, such as mounts, and other attaching parts for equipment designated for removal from "T" prefixed aircraft will not be included in these lists and will not be removed when any aircraft is stripped or modified for training purposes.

14. **Headquarters USAF.** Headquarters USAF will approve bulk reclassification of aircraft (including line of aircraft) by type, model, series, and block number in accordance with the latest modernization policies and tactical considerations.

15. **Modification and Redesignation Policy:**

a. "Z" classified aircraft may be stripped of miscellaneous armament, photographic, communication, oxygen, and navigational equipment not required in the specific mission assignment of the aircraft. The removal of this equipment is subject only to the approval of the commanding general of the command under which the aircraft is assigned. This authority does not include the removal of any installation provisions, such as mounts, brackets, or other attaching parts for equipment or the installation of equipment other than that authorized for installation in the aircraft at the time of its classification as "Z" aircraft. Authority to install additional equipment in "Z" aircraft will be obtained in accordance with paragraph 9.

b. "T" designated and "T" prefixed aircraft may be stripped of miscellaneous armament, photographic, communication, oxygen, and navigational equipment not required in the specific mission assignment of the aircraft. Removal of this equipment is subject only to the approval of the commanding general of the command to which the aircraft is assigned. This authority does not include the removal of any installation provisions, such as mounts, brackets,

6   8-7370, AF

AFR 65-60
15-17

or other attaching parts for equipment or the installation of equipment other than that authorized for installation by applicable directives for the specific "T" designated or "T" prefixed aircraft. Authority to install additional equipment in "T" designated or "T" prefixed aircraft will be obtained in accordance with paragraph 9.

c. Modification undertaken by the Air Materiel Command will, in general, be only that work beyond the capabilities of the operating activity possessing the aircraft. If necessary, in the interest of expediting completion of projects, the Air Materiel Command may make arrangements with other commands for assistance. All such work thus accomplished will be under the general supervision of and in accordance with technical instructions furnished by the Air Materiel Command. Modifications undertaken by commands other than the Air Materiel Command will be in accordance with Air Materiel Command approved drawings or technical instructions.

d. Equipment removed from aircraft in accordance with paragraphs 10b and b above, will be stored by the activity to which the aircraft is assigned and reinstalled prior to the transfer of the aircraft.

e. Aircraft modified in accordance with paragraphs 10a and b will not require redesignation.

f. Aircraft modified in accordance with paragraphs 10c and 11, when interchangeability of the aircraft with like type, model, series, and block aircraft has been affected, will be redesignated as "E" aircraft.

16. **Statistical Grouping.** For purposes of statistical grouping of types of aircraft the following principles will be followed:

a. All aircraft with basic type designator only will always be classed under the basic type, e.g., B-50A-10: Bomber Type.

b. All aircraft with the basic type designator prefixed by another designator authorized as a prefix symbol excluding the prefixes "D," "M," and "V" ("B," "C," "F," "G," "L," "Q," "R," "S," and "T"), will always be classed under the type indicated by the primary prefix, e.g., ERB-50A-10: Reconnaissance Type.

17. **TO 01-1-81.** Appropriate implementing instructions for this Regulation are contained in Technical Order 01-1-81.

BY ORDER OF THE SECRETARY OF THE AIR FORCE:

HOYT S. VANDENBERG
Chief of Staff, United States Air Force

OFFICIAL:

E. E. TORO
Colonel, USAF
Acting Air Adjutant General

DISTRIBUTION:
D; G

83

b. IDENTIFICATION MARKINGS.

(1) On all fighter, trainer, and light bombardment type aircraft except those of the National Guard, an identification marking will be placed on each side of the fuselage if space permits without relocation of the insignia. These identification markings will consist of two letters and three numerals determined as outlined in the following instructions. Letters and numerals will be of uniform size, with the letters separated from the numerals by a dash. If any duplication of identification symbols should occur on permanently assigned aircraft at any one installation, a suffix letter may be used to further identify the aircraft. The suffix letter will be of a size and so placed so that the size of the basic identification symbol is not reduced.

(2) The location of the fuselage markings will depend upon the fuselage surface available therefor. They will be the largest size practicable, determined

by available space; however, in no case will they be smaller than 8 x 12 inches, or larger than 32 x 48 inches. The proportion of width and length of the stroke, to the height will be the same as that of wing markings insofar as practicable.

(3) Identification markings will be yellow on camouflaged surfaces and black on aluminized surfaces, and of either gloss or lustreless enamel or lacquer. Black camouflaged aircraft will have insignia red identification markings.

(4) The first letter of the identification marking will identify the type of aircraft, the second letter will be an equivalent for the model number and the numerals will be the last three numerals of the serial number. The letters to be used for the various types and models, together with an example of the identification markings of a specific aircraft of each type are set forth below:

LETTER DESIGNATION FOR TYPE	MODEL	LETTER EQUIVALENT FOR MODEL	
Light Bombardment Aircraft			
B	26	C	EXAMPLE: On B-26B, AF No. 43-22465, the identification marking would be BC-465.
B	25	D	
B	45	E	
Fighter Aircraft			
F	38	A	EXAMPLE: On F-38J, AF No. 42-67126 the identification marking would be FA-126.
F	47	E	
F	51	F	
F	59	J	
F	61	K	
F	63	L	
F	80	T	
F	81	P	
F	82	Q	
F	83	R	
F	84	S	
Trainer Aircraft			
T	AT-6	A	EXAMPLE: On T-11, AF No. 42-36867, the identification marking would be TC-867.
T	AT-7	B	
T	AT-11	C	
BT	BT-13	E	
PT	PT-13	F	
T	PT-17	G	
T	PT-19	H	
Q	PQ-14	K	

c. Radio call numbers are not required on primary trainers which do not have radio equipment and which bear field identifying numbers; however, identification markings required by paragraph 4.b., of this Section, are applicable to primary trainers.

d. AIR FORCE MARKINGS.

(1) All of the markings described in the following paragraphs 4.d.(2) to (5) inclusive consist of vertical block type lettering and will be yellow on camouflaged surfaces and black on aluminized surfaces and of either

gloss or lustreless enamel or lacquer. Black camouflaged aircraft will have insignia red identification markings.

(2) The letters "USAF" will be placed on the lower surface of the left wing and upper surface of the right wing of all USAF aircraft. The height and location of this marking will correspond with the national insignia presently on the opposite wing of the aircraft concerned. Width of the letters will be two-thirds the height, width of strokes one-sixth the height and with spacing one-sixth the height. The top of the letters will be toward the leading edge of the wing.

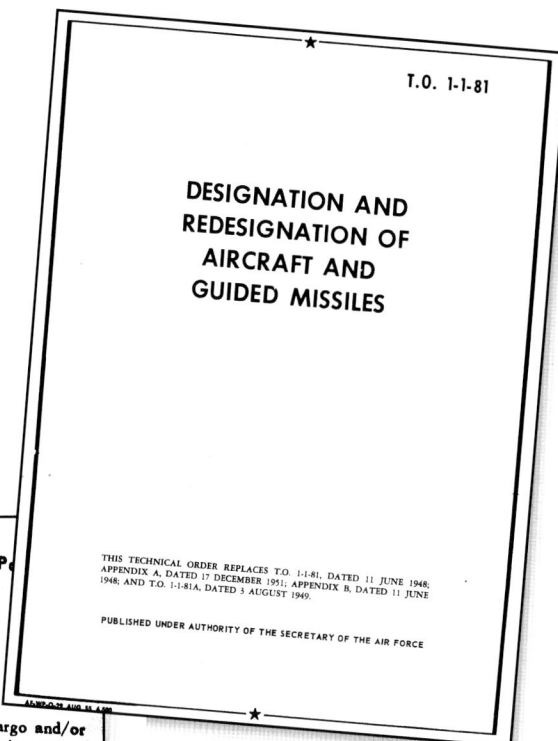

T.O. 1-1-81

DESIGNATION AND
REDESIGNATION OF
AIRCRAFT AND
GUIDED MISSILES

THIS TECHNICAL ORDER REPLACES T.O. 1-1-81, DATED 11 JUNE 1948; APPENDIX A, DATED 17 DECEMBER 1951; APPENDIX B, DATED 11 JUNE 1948; AND T.O. 1-1-81A, DATED 5 AUGUST 1949.

PUBLISHED UNDER AUTHORITY OF THE SECRETARY OF THE AIR FORCE

T.O. 1-1-81

TABLE II
AIRCRAFT PREFIX LETTERS

LETTER	TITLE	DESCRIPTION
C	Transport	Aircraft designed primarily for the purpose of carrying cargo and/or passengers. Aircraft having this type letter will be those having a payload capacity of the basic mission greater than 2000 lbs.
D	Director	Aircraft capable of controlling a drone aircraft or a guided missile. Example: DF-80, DB-17.
E	Early Warning	Aircraft having electronic devices to permit employment as an early warning radar station. Example: EC-121C, EB-29.
G	Carrier	Aircraft capable of carrying or storing within the aircraft a parasite type aerial vehicle. Example: GB-36.
K	Tanker	Aircraft having special equipment to provide in-flight refueling of other aircraft. Example: KB-29.
M	Medical	Aircraft having equipment such as litters, galleys, heated blanket outlets and special oxygen outlets and which are specifically intended for transportation of medical patients.
P	Passenger	Aircraft having permanent structural provisions for the transportation of passengers and which cannot be readily modified at base level for the conversion of the aircraft to carry cargo.
Q	Drone	Aircraft capable of being controlled from a point outside the aircraft. Example: QB-17, QF-80.
R	Reconnaissance	Aircraft having equipment permanently installed for photographic and/or electronic reconnaissance missions. Example: RB-47, RF-101.
S	Search Rescue	Aircraft having special equipment for performance of search and rescue missions. Example: SB-29.
T	Training	Aircraft having training equipment installed for purposes of conducting training missions. Example: TC-54, TB-50.
V	Staff	Aircraft having accomodations such as chairs, tables, lounge, berths, etc, for the transportation of staff personnel. Example: VC-121, VC-131.
W	Weather	Aircraft having meteorological equipment permanently installed. Example: WB-29, WB-50. Aircraft used for weather reconnaissance without inclusion of permanently installed meteorological equipment will not be designated by the prefix "W".

(1) A change is made in the engine which materially affects the performance rating or precludes or affects interchangeability of engines in an aircraft. (Specific examples: – Change from reciprocating to turbo-prop engine – C-121A, R3350-75 to YC-121F, T-34-P-6.)

(2) A change is made in propellers which precludes or affects interchangeability (Curtiss instead of Hamilton Standard) or flying characteristics of an aircraft (13ft-6in. propeller instead of a 12ft-6in. propeller).

(3) A major change in primary installed armament. (Addition or relocation of turrets, addition or deletion of guns, installation of 20 mm guns in place of .50 cal guns, etc.)

b. Series changes will be assigned the next consecutive alphabetic designation above the last assigned series letter of a specific type and model. To avoid confusion, the letters "I" and "O" will not be used as series letters.

7. MANUFACTURER'S CODE.

The letters denoting the prime contractor of an aircraft will be placed following the series letters (or the model number, if a series letter is not applicable). Two letters will be used to represent the prime contractor of the aircraft. A listing of the manufacturers' codes is included as Appendix A to this technical order.

T.O. 1-1-81

TABLE III

AIRCRAFT COMPONENT ASSIGNMENT LETTERS

US AIR FORCE.. A
US ARMY .... G
AIR NATIONAL GUARD .... N
AIR RESERVE .... R
ROTC .... T

TABLE IV
AIRCRAFT CLASSIFICATION LETTERS

TITLE	DESCRIPTION
Special Test, Temporary	Aircraft on special test by authorized organizations and aircraft on bailment contract, whose installed property has been temporarily removed to accomodate the test. The aircraft are exempt from compliance with technical orders for the period of the test, except immediate action and urgent action technical orders, which will be complied with upon receipt, or in the time allowed. Technical orders not complied with will be entered on appropriate forms and paragraph 12.a., Section II of T.O. 1-1-81 will be shown as the reason for non-compliance. All technical orders so entered will be complied with at completion of the test and the aircraft will be returned to the basic configuration at time of initial receipt for test.
Special Test	Aircraft on special test projects by authorized activities and aircraft on bailment contract whose configuration is drastically changed so that return of the aircraft to its original configuration is beyond practicable or economical limits. Installed property removed for test will be returned to stock in accordance with applicable publications and aircraft forms corrected to reflect removals. These aircraft are exempt from all technical order compliance, including immediate and urgent action technical orders, which will be accomplished at the discretion of the possessing command. Technical orders complied with will be entered on appropriate forms, and the aircraft will be returned to the Air Materiel Command for disposal at the completion of the test. This classification letter will be assigned only upon prior approval of HQ, USAF.
Experimental	Aircraft in a developmental, experimental stage where basic type and model has been designed but not established as a standard aircraft for service use.
Prototype	Aircraft procured in limited quantities to develop the potentialities of the model. Normally these aircraft will be produced on experimental tooling and will remain in test status for the life of the aircraft. (Aircraft procured for development tests and produced on production tooling will be designated by the basic type and model. At such time as these aircraft are modified to a standard production configuration they will be redesignated appropriately. Example: T-37, redesignated to T-37A.)

T.O. 1-1-636

3-17. AMC depots will replace command and organizational insignia and markings which are included in major air command written directives when aircraft are undergoing IRAN or modification either in AMC depot shops or under AMC contract.

3-18. No specific locations for organizational insignia and markings are mandatory but points between the wing and tail surfaces on opposite sides of the fuselage are considered most desirable. In no case will size of insignia exceed 50 percent of height of fuselage at point of application. Similar aircraft in the same organization will have the same size insignia. If applied to other than smooth surfaces, insignia may be painted on aluminum sheet which is bolted or screwed securely to rigid members of the aircraft.

3-19. Command or organizational identification lettering in no case will exceed ½ the size of the US AIR FORCE distinguishing markings.

3-20. IDENTIFICATION MARKINGS.

3-21. Identification markings will be placed on each side of the fuselage of all types and models of fighter, trainer, light bombardment, and liaison aircraft including those assigned to overseas theaters but excepting those of the National Guard and Department of the Army. These identification markings are to be placed on aircraft to prevent BUZZING and will consist of two letters and three numerals determined as outlined in the following instructions. Letters and numerals will be of uniform size, with the letters separated from the numerals by a dash. If any duplication of identification symbols should occur on permanently assigned aircraft at any one installation, a suffix letter may be used to further identify the aircraft. The suffix letter will be of a size and so placed that the size of the basic identification symbol is not reduced. Aircraft identification markings should be uniform on similar type aircraft in each organization.

3-22. The location of the fuselage markings will depend upon the fuselage surface available. They will be the largest size practicable, determined by available space; however, in no case will they be smaller than 8 x 12 inches, or larger than 32 x 48 inches. The proportion of width and length of the stroke to the height will be the same as that of wing markings insofar as practicable.

3-23. Identification markings will be insignia-blue on aluminized surfaces. Jet black may be used if insignia-blue is unavailable. Identification markings will be insignia-red on a black finish.

3-24. The first letter of the identification marking will identify the type of aircraft, the second letter will be an equivalent of the model number and the numerals will be the last three figures of the serial number. The letters to be used for the various types and models, together with an example of the identification markings of a specific aircraft of each type, are indicated in Table II.

3-25. RADIO CALL NUMBERS.

3-26. Radio call numbers of not less than five numerals will be maintained on all USAF aircraft except primary trainers which do not have radio equipment and which bear field identifying numbers. However, identification markings required by paragraph 3-20 are to be placed on primary trainers. The radio call numbers will be applied to both sides or each outboard side, as applicable, of the vertical stabilizer and rudder assembly, except that on rotary winged aircraft they will be applied to the sides of the fuselage. These call numbers, or designators, will be of a size discernible at a distance of 150 yards. The suggested minimum size is 8 inches wide and 12 inches high, but if numbers this size cannot be applied due to lack of space, they will be made as large as possible. On medium and heavy bombardment aircraft and on all other four-engined aircraft, numerals for radio call markings will be 18 inches in height. Radio call numbers will be derived from the aircraft serial number. The first numeral of the contract year and the hyphen in the aircraft serial number will not be used in the radio call number. If five numerals are not available, zeros will be used to fill-in to five numerals. EXAMPLE: Radio call number for aircraft serial No. 51-7 will be 10007. Should more than five numerals be available, they should be used if there is sufficient space. Where space is available for only five numerals, the last five numerals of the aircraft serial number will be used. Insignia-blue numerals will be used on aluminized surfaces and insignia-red numerals will be used on a black finish. Jet black may be used if insignia-blue is unavailable. Decalcomanias are authorized if available.

NOTE

Where aircraft are 10 years old, there is a possibility that two sets of radio call numbers could be identical. To prevent this, the symbol 0- will precede radio call numbers derived from serial numbers which are 10 years old.

3-27. PROPELLER MARKINGS.

3-28. American propeller blades, design numbers A-2721107, A-2891100, and A-2891106, used in sets in Aeroproducts propellers, and design numbers, C-2721200 and C-3821306, used in sets in Curtiss propellers, respectively, will be identified by a yellow stripe ⅜-inch in width and ⅜-inch inboard of the yellow tip. A. O. Smith propeller blades, design number prefix SPA, used in sets in Curtiss propellers will be identified by two ⅜-inch yellow stripes, one ⅜-inch inboard of the yellow tip and the other ⅜-inch inboard from the first. These stripes will extend completely around the blade section. The stenciled markings between the 18 and 24-inch stations in the cambered side of the propeller blades will be retained. When the exact location of the blade reference station

39

TABLE II

LETTER DESIGNATION FOR TYPE	MODEL	LETTER EQUIVALENT FOR MODEL	
	Light Bombardment Aircraft		
B			
B	26	C	
B	25	D	
B	45	E	EXAMPLE: On B-26B, AF No. 43-22465, the identification marking would be BC-465.
B	57	A	
B	66	B	
	Fighter Aircraft		
F	51		
F	80	F	EXAMPLE: On F-94, AF No. 49-67126, the identification marking would be FA-126.
F	84	T	
F	86	S	
F	89	U	
F	94	V	
F	100	A	
F	101	W	
F	102	B	
F	103	C	
F	104	D	
F	105	G	
	Trainer Aircraft	H	
T	6		
T	7	A	
T	11	B	EXAMPLE: On T-11, AF No. 42-36867, the identification marking would be TC-867.
T	28	C	
T	33	L	
T	34	R	
T	37	D	
	Liaison Aircraft	E	
L	4		
L	5	A	
L	16	B	EXAMPLE: On L-20, AF No. 52-6079, the identification marking would be LG-079.
L	17	C	
L	18	D	
L	19	E	
L	20	F	
L	21	G	
L	23	H	
L	26	J	
		K	

is known, a stripe of yellow paint ⅛-inch wide, 2 inches long, and spaced equidistant between the leading and trailing edge of the blade will be placed on the thrust face of the reference station. Unless the exact location of the reference station on the blade is known, no attempt will be made to identify this location by the aforementioned stripe.

3-29. HELICOPTER ROTOR BLADE MARKINGS.

3-30. Classification numbers will be stenciled on the main rotor blades of all helicopters by any facility authorized to balance or alter the blade. Three numbers will be utilized; the first will be the weight in

pounds of the blade expressed in decimal form; the second will be the distance in inches from the center of rotation to the center of gravity of the blade; the third number will be the distance in inches from the leading edge of the blade to the center of gravity of the blade chord-wise. EXAMPLE: 57.2-75.5-5.2, when the blade has a weight of 57.2 pounds with the center of gravity 75.5 inches from the center of rotation, and the chordwise center of gravity is 5.2 inches from the leading edge of the blade. Stenciling, approximately ¾-inch in height, will be accomplished with a paint or dope which contrasts well with the color of the blade. The preceding information is to be

40

or corrosion-resistant purposes, it will be applied by spraying the hub and each propeller blade while they are in a horizontal position, and retaining the propeller in this position until the paint materials have set. Over one light coat of zinc chromate primer, Specification MIL-P-6889, one light coat of cellulose nitrate black lustreless lacquer, Specification MIL-L-6805, will be applied and will extend to within 4 inches of the tip of the blade; this 4-inch tip section will receive one light coat of cellulose nitrate yellow lustreless lacquer, Specification MIL-L-6805, Color MIDDLESTONE, Color No. 615. The propeller will then be checked for balance. Care will be exercised to mask any angular graduations on the propeller hub or blades. The space between the blade shank and barrel will be masked off to prevent paint from contacting the seals.

2-32. When necessary, three and four blade metal propellers may be lightly touched up between overhaul periods while installed on the aircraft. Care will be exercised to apply proportionate amounts of paint to each blade to maintain proper blade balance. Where anti-glare paint can be applied to all blades of a propeller assembly in proportionate amounts, propeller balance need not be accomplished. This is not to be interpreted as authorization for deletion of propeller balance at overhaul or at any other time when balance is normally required. (Refer to paragraph 3-27, for markings.)

2-33. Helicopter main rotor blades will be aluminized when recovering or major repair is necessary. (Refer to paragraph 3-29, for markings.)

2-34. To promote ground safety, all helicopter tail-rotor blades except Sikorsky blades utilizing B and B bonding and having vinyl plastic tape installed will be marked as follows:

a. Prime surface with one light coat of zinc chromate primer, Specification MIL-P-6889.

b. Apply a 6-inch band of bright red lacquer, Specification MIL-L-6805, Color No. 619, to the tail rotor tip, followed by a 6-inch band of insignia-white lacquer, Specification MIL-L-7178, Color No. 511, and another 6-inch band of bright red lacquer.

c. Following the second band of bright red lacquer, Specification MIL-L-6805, Color No. 619, a band of black lacquer, Specification MIL-L-6805, Color No. 604, will be applied up to within 6 inches of the hub.

d. The remaining 6 inches of the tail rotor blade will be painted with bright red lacquer, Specification MIL-L-6805, Color No. 619.

NOTE

To avoid the possibility of unbalanced conditions, application of the color scheme outlined above will be limited to new blades or to overhauled blades. Only contractors or overhaul agencies will apply these markings to the tail rotor blades of USAF helicopters.

2-35. FINISH FOR AIRCRAFT OPERATED IN THE COLD WEATHER AREA.

2-36. Aircraft assigned to operate during any period of the year, in or through that portion of the cold weather area, beyond the limit of the zone of the interior (refer to T.O. 00-60A-1), will have the designated external surface areas finished in insignia-red enamel or lacquer conforming to Specification MIL-E-7729 or MIL-L-7178 respectively. These coatings will be applied over zinc chromate primer, Specification MIL-P-6889. These markings will facilitate observation of ground borne aircraft in the event of a forced or crash landing, regardless of the attitude of the aircraft after coming to rest.

2-37. All USAF aircraft assigned to operate in or through the cold weather area during any period of the year will have designated external surfaces finished in insignia-red, Specification MIL-E-7729 or MIL-L-7178, Color No. 509, except those aircraft specifically exempted by Hq USAF, Rescue, Air Attache and aircraft on a tactical mission operating in arctic regions for periods of 90 days or less. Arctic marking of aircraft will be accomplished prior to arrival at the aerial port of embarkation. Aircraft scheduled for one-time flight through or into and return from a designated portion of cold weather area over established air routes are exempt from this requirement.

2-38. Leading and tip edges of airfoil sections located within an area to be arctic finished will be exempt from painting due to wind blast deterioration of paint. The upper and lower edges of metal airfoil will determine the areas exempt from arctic finish provided such boundaries do not extend more than 12 inches aft of the center line of a wing leading edge, and not more than 6 inches aft of the center line of a stabilizer leading edge. In the interest of appearance, these dimensions should be tapered as the leading edge nears and joins the tip edge of the wing or stabilizer.

2-39. The surface of a fabric covered flight control located within the area to be arctic finished will be excluded therefrom, unless the airfoil panel to which the control attaches is also fabric covered.

2-40. All standard AF aircraft insignia and markings and other approved markings and coding authorized to appear within an area to be arctic finished will be located as directed by applicable publications. A three-inch border will be allowed to exist between large insignia or markings and the arctic finish. A relatively smaller border will be allowed to exist between insignia or markings.

2-41. Antenna masts, loops and housing located within the area to be arctic finished will be exempt from being painted insignia-red. Wing de-icers will also be exempt, including heated sections of wing and tail surfaces.

2-42. The designated areas to be covered by the distinctive finish for arctic operated aircraft will be as follows:

a. FIXED WING AIRCRAFT.

(1) WING.

(a) Apply an insignia-red finish to the upper and lower surfaces of the outer wing sections.

(b) The area of each outer wing section to be arctic finished depends on the chord of the wing through a span distance inboard from each wing tip equal to approximately 25 percent of the wing span called out under DESCRIPTION, DIMENSIONS, AND LEADING PARTICULARS in the applicable maintenance handbook for the type and model aircraft affected.

(2) FUSELAGE. Apply an insignia-red finish, Specification MIL-E-7729 or MIL-L-7178, Color No.

509, to the entire aft portion of the fuselage from the tip of the tail forward for a distance equal to approximately 25 percent of the total fuselage length.

(3) EMPENNAGE. Apply an insignia-red finish to both sides of the stabilizers, including metal control surfaces attached thereto.

b. ROTARY WING AIRCRAFT. An insignia-red finish will be applied to the external metal or fabric surface and to exposed structural frame work of the aft portion of the fuselage equal to approximately 40 percent of the total external area of the fuselage. Exclude main and tail rotors, exposed portions of operating mechanism, transparent panels and radio antenna equipment.

SECTION III

USAF STANDARD AIRCRAFT INSIGNIA AND MARKINGS

3-1. USAF STANDARD INSIGNIA.

3-2. GENERAL DESCRIPTION.

a. The standard national star insignia of the design, shown in figure 1, will be placed on all USAF aircraft. It will be applied so that in normal flight attitude of the aircraft, the top point of the star of the insignia points upward on fuselage surfaces and forward on wing surfaces. On aircraft having swept wings or wings of variable sweep, the national insignia will be placed so that it will not extend into flaps, slats, or control surfaces, provided the specified size and symmetry are maintained. The line through the top point of the star and its center will be perpendicular to the line formed by the constant 50 percent chord line of the wing, which passes through the center of the star.

b. The diameter of the blue circle (excluding the border) will be in multiples of 5 inches. EXAMPLE: 20, 25, 30, 35, etc.

c. The standard insignia (see figure 1) will be an insignia-white five pointed star inside an insignia-blue circumscribed circle with an insignia-white rectangle. The length of the rectangle shall be one radius of the blue circle and the width shall be ½ of the radius of the blue circle. The rectangle shall be placed on each side of the star so that the top edges will form a straight line with the top edges of the two points beneath the top point of the star. An insignia-red horizontal stripe shall be centered in the white rectangle at each side of the star; the width of the red stripe is to be ⅙ of the radius of the blue circle. An insignia-blue border, width being ⅛ of the radius of the blue circle, will outline the entire design. When the insignia is to be applied on a sea blue, dark blue or

black background, the insignia-blue circle and the insignia-blue border may be omitted.

3-3. WING INSIGNIA. The diameter of the blue circle (excluding the border) will be the standard size which is the nearest to, but does not exceed, 75 percent of the distance between the edge of the wing and the aileron cut-out at the point of application. The diameter of the blue circle (excluding the border) will not be greater than 60 inches or less than 30 inches. The insignia, specified herein, will be placed on the top surface of the left wing and on the lower surface of the right wing with the center of the insignia inboard from each wing tip. The insignia will be ⅓ of the distance from the wing tip to the fuselage, and with the blue border touching the aileron cut-out. The insignia may be moved in a minimum distance necessary where space is not available for the minimum size specified. On bi-planes, the insignia will be applied only to the upper left wing and lower right wing.

3-4. FUSELAGE INSIGNIA. The diameter of the blue circle (excluding the border) will be the standard size which is nearest to, but not greater than 75 percent of the height of the fuselage at the point of application. The diameter of the blue circle (excluding the border) will be not less than 20 inches or greater than 50 inches. These will be placed and maintained on each side of the fuselage (near midway) between the trailing edge of the wing and leading edge of the horizontal stabilizer, but may be moved to the rear, or forward, of the midpoint to avoid turrets or other plastic material. The insignia may extend over doors and emergency exits, but shall not extend over windows or openings which would change the insignia pattern. If the fuselage section, as de-

6

the second numeral of the aircraft contract year (omitting the hyphen) shall then be used, followed by necessary quantities of zeroes to produce five numerals.

EXAMPLE:

The radio call number of aircraft Serial Number 59-12A would be 90012.

d. All radio call number placards installed within aircraft, including helicopters, shall reflect the same radio call number as applied on the aircraft exterior.

NOTE

To avoid possible duplication of radio call numbers of new aircraft and aircraft at least 10 years old, the symbol 0- shall precede all radio call numbers on aircraft 10 years and older (i. e. 0-25123). This requirement is also applicable to the radio call number placard on the instrument panel. Age of the aircraft is to be determined by contract serial number without regard to when it was accepted by the Air Force. In those cases where the surface area of the vertical fin does not permit the addition of the prefix 0- in the prescribed size numerals, the next smaller size numerals in increments of 3 inches is authorized. For example: Radio call numbers on F-104 aircraft should normally be 12 inches high; when the requirement for the addition of the 0- prefix exists, 9 inch numerals may be used, if necessary.

3-21. MISSILE IDENTIFICATION NUMBER.

a. Missile identification number markings for USAF missiles are similar in makeup to those for aircraft radio call numbers. Missile identification numbers shall be placed and maintained on each side of the vertical fin or guide vane on USAF missiles. Missiles which do not incorporate fins or guide vanes will have the missile identification number applied to the aft fuselage.

b. On horizontally viewed missiles the fuselage missile identification number will be applied on a plane at right angles to the U.S. AIR FORCE marking or missile longitudinal center line.

c. The identification number shall be placed on each stage of multi-stage missiles.

d. The missile identification marking shall consist of five numerals derived from the missile serial numbers. Arabic numerals will be used when applying missile identification numbers.

e. The first numeral of the contract year and the hyphen in the missile serial number shall not be used in the missile identification number.

f. If five numerals are not available in the missile serial number from which to derive the required five numerals for an identification marking, zeroes will be used to produce five numerals. Example: The missile identification marking for missile serial number 58-7 will be 80007.

g. Should more than five numerals be available, the last five numerals of the missile serial number will be used. Example: The identification marking for missile serial number 58-968574 will be: 68574.

3-22. GENERAL SPECIFICATION FOR LETTERING AND NUMERALS USED IN MARKING FOR AIRCRAFT AND MISSILES.

3-23. Vertical block (Chamfered Gothic) type letters and arabic numerals should be used when applying markings on aircraft and missiles. (See Appendix A for construction of letters and numerals Unless otherwise specified herein, insignia-blue, Color No. 15044, will be used for letters and numerals applied on gray or white surfaces. Gloss black, Color No. 17038, may be used as a substitute for the insignia-blue. Insignia-white, Color No. 17875, will be used on red finishes. Insignia-red, Color No. 11136, will be used on block finishes. Use Specification MIL-L-19537 acrylic nitrocellulose lacquer; however, TT-E-489 enamel may be used only for maintenance or touch up of insignia and markings on aircraft presently painted with an enamel system still in good condition.

3-24. IDENTIFICATION OF PAINT SHOP AND THE APPLIED FINISH.

a. All aircraft receiving a paint finish on the exterior surfaces, the contractor or activity performing the work shall apply markings consisting of a circular patch approximately 2 1/2 to 4 inch in diameter. The patch shall be located on the right side of the fuselage, on the underside and even with the leading edge of the horizontal stabilizer or delta wing. This marking shall contain the following information.

(1) Contractor or overhaul activity Federal Manufacturer's code. (If no code exists, name and address).

(2) Date of completion of paint application (month, day, year).

(3) Identification by specification number of every coating of the general system applied to the exterior of the aircraft.

AIR FORCE REGULATION
NO. 66–11
ARMY REGULATIONS
NO. 700–26
BUWEPS INSTRUCTION 13100.7

AFR 66–11
AR 700–26
BUWEPS INSTRUCTION 13100.7

DEPARTMENTS OF THE AIR FORCE, THE ARMY,
AND THE NAVY
Washington, *18 September 1962*

5/5 by AFR 66-11, 8 Feb 68

Depot, Field and Organizational Maintenance

DESIGNATING, REDESIGNATING, AND NAMING MILITARY AIRCRAFT

This regulation establishes uniform procedures, authority and responsibilities for designating, redesignating, and naming military aircraft. It implements DOD Directive 4505.6, 6 July 1962.

	Paragraph
Scope and Applicability	1
Explanation of Terms	2
Designation System	3
Designation and Redesignation of Aircraft	4
Naming of Aircraft	5
Responsibilities	6
Assignment of Aircraft Designators	7

1. Scope and Applicability. The designation system described herein covers all current and newly designed aircraft (fixed, movable, and rotary wing) and airships, and is applicable to all elements of the military departments.

2. Explanation of Terms:

a. *Aircraft.* A heavier-than-air vehicle, designed primarily for flight in the atmosphere, which has incorporated in its prime design the ability and/or requirement for human occupancy.

b. *Basic Mission Symbol.* A letter used to indicate the prime intended function or capability of the aircraft, such as a bomber, fighter, patrol, etc.

~~c. *Design Number.* The sequence number of~~ each new design of the same basic mission or type aircraft.

d. *Modified Mission Symbol.* A letter used to indicate the current capability of an aircraft or airship when it is so modified that its orginal intended capability is no longer applicable, or when it has an added or restricted capability.

c. *Series Letter.* A letter used to denote difference affecting methods of employment, differences affecting relation of the vehicle to its ground environment, and major modifications to the aircraft or airship which result in significant changes to the logistic support.

f. *Type.* A letter which designates an airship or an aircraft other than fixed-wing.

3. Designation System. The designation system shall consist of a combination of significant letters and numbers as follows:

a. *Status Prefix Symbol.* The status letter, if applicable, will indicate aircraft or airship being used for experimentation and special or service test. Attachment 1 contains status letters authorized for use. The status letter will be placed at the immediate left of the modified mission letter or the mission/type symbols if no modified mission letter is applicable.

b. *Modified Mission Symbol.* The modified mission symbol will consist of a prefix letter placed at the immediate left of the basic mission or type letter. Each military department will determine the need for the assignment of a prefix letter. Attachment 2 contains the modified mission symbols authorized for use.

c. *Basic Mission and Type Symbols.* A basic mission letter is used to denote the primary function or capability of an aircraft. Mission/type symbols denote the mission and type of aircraft other than fixed-wing. An aircraft identified by a type symbol such as "H" for helicopter, will be further identified by only one mission symbol whether it be the basic mission or a modified mission symbol. Attachment 3 contains the basic mission and type symbols authorized for use.

This regulation supersedes AR 705–42, 21 March 1957/BUWEPSINST 13100.1A, 17 May 1961.

OPI: AFSSV
DISTRIBUTION: S
(For Army and Navy distribution, see page 4.)

AFR 66–11
AR 700–26
BUWEPS INSTRUCTION 13100.7

EXCEPTION: The designation of R/S as the basic mission symbol for integrated reconnaissance strike capability.

d. *Design Number.* A number will be assigned for each basic mission or type. New design numbers will be assigned when an existing aircraft or airship is redesigned to an extent that it no longer reflects the original configuration or capability. Examples of changes requiring design redesignations on aircraft are as follows:

(1) Changing the number of engines of a specific aircraft.

(2) Changing the wing or control surface design of a specific aircraft from a straight wing to a swept or delta wing design.

(3) Changing the empennage of a specific design from straight to swept surfaces or relocating the empennage.

e. *Series Symbol.* A letter will be assigned to each series change of a specific basic design. To avoid confusion the letter "I" and "O" will not be used as series letters. In designating new aircraft, the series letter will be in consecutive order starting with "A."

f. *Source or Manfacturer's Code.* A two letter code will be used to identify the prime or assembly contractor. Attachment 4 contains source or manufacturer's codes currently authorized for use.

g. *Block Numbers.* The production block numbering system will consist of the assignment of production blocks, starting at 01, next 05, and progressing in multiples of 5 after 05. Intermediate block numbers are reserved for field modifications and will be applied by the using military department.

h. *Serial Number.* The method of assignment of serial numbers will be at the discretion of the using military department.

i. *Basic Designation.* The basic designation will consist of items a-e as applicable, in the order shown. A dash (—) will be inserted between the basic mission/type symbol and the design number.

4. Designation and Redesignation of Aircraft:

a. All Department of Defense aircraft have been assigned designations to conform with the provisions of these regulations. The cross-reference list contained in attachment 5 shows the current designation for each of these aircraft.

former designation, and the applicable military department. New aircraft will be assigned the next consecutive design number within each basic mission/type, except for those in the bomber, cargo/transport, and fighter categories; the designations for these latter aircraft will begin with "B–1A," "C–3A," and "F–12A" respectively. In connection with the redesignation of aircraft, the minimum effort required for efficient operations will be expended. For example:

(1) Complete document conversion will be delayed until a publication, drawing, etc., undergoes revision for some other cause.

(2) To the extent practicable, essential document changes will be made in pen and ink, and new cover pages for technical publications and manuals will be substituted for old ones.

(3) Extensive use will be made of cross-reference lists showing the former and current designations.

b. The above-mentioned redesignations are effective upon publication of these regulations, and will be implemented as soon as possible.

5. Naming of Aircraft. The following precepts shall be observed in assigning popular names to military aircraft:

a. Only those which have reached the production stage, or have immediate prospects of going into production, will be assigned popular names.

b. Popular names will normally (1) consist of one word, for purposes of brevity, and (2) be selected to conform to characteristics of the aircraft.

c. Popular names will not supplant designations and will not duplicate those in use for other types of material, such as tanks, etc.

d. To avoid duplication, each popular name under consideration will be checked against the master list of popular names maintained by the Industrial Branch, Office of Information, Office of the Secretary of the Air Force (SAFOI-2b).

e. Each basic model will normally retain the popular name originally assigned, regardless of its subsequent manufacturer or operational use. All aircraft of a series within a basic mission and type will retain the one popular name assigned thereto.

f. A "family" of popular names for future models may be reserved for the exclusive use of the manufacturer on request, upon unanimous agreement among the military departments.

2

6. Responsibilities:

a. The Department of the Air Force will: (1) maintain the designation system and assign all new designations; (2) maintain a current list of popular names assigned to military aircraft and, insofar as practicable, the names of civil and foreign aircraft; (3) maintain a list of currently assigned designations, and the popular names associated therewith, and issue a revised attachment 5 to these regulations at regular intervals; and (4) maintain a current list of source or manufacturer's codes, and issue revisions to attachment 4 of these regulations to provide additions or deletions as appropriate.

b. Each military department will: (1) assign popular names to its military aircraft in accordance with the precepts of paragraph 5 and advise the Department of the Air Force, and (2) coordinate with the Department of the Air Force on authorized changes to all attachments to these regulations.

7. Assignment of Aircraft Designators:

a. The single point of contact within the requesting service will initiate a request and forward to the assignment agency. The request may be in the form of a letter, TWX, or other appropriate media. The request will include a description of the aircraft, intended use, the manufacturer's identification thereof, and other information considered pertinent by the requestor.

b. The requesting service will indicate the desired mission or type symbols. The assignment agency will assign the applicable design number and/or the applicable series letter.

c. When necessary, the requesting agency may request a designation assignment from the assignment agency by telephone. Such requests will be followed-up immediately by a written request.

d. The requesting agency will submit a separate designation request for each series letter assignment desired. All series letter assignments will be made by the assignment agency to preclude duplication among the three services.

AFR 66–11
AR 700–26
BUWEPS INSTRUCTION 13100.7

e. The requesting agency will assign status and modified mission prefixes as necessary. It will not be necessary to request these from the assignment agency; however, immediately upon such assignments, the requesting agency will notify the assignment agency for record and publication purposes. In the event a new series letter or model number is required in conjunction with the proposed modification, these will be requested from the assignment agency in the same manner as for new designs or normal new series changes.

f. Periodically (not less frequently than every 6 months) the assignment agency will publish an unclassified listing of assigned designations. The list will include the complete designation, responsible service, and a short unclassified description. This publication will be distributed in accordance with a list to be established by the three services and furnished to the assignment agency.

g. Internal administration of the assignment or requesting agency for a particular service (whichever is applicable) will be the responsibility of that particular service.

h. Single point of contact in each of the three services:

AIR FORCE: Aeronautical Systems Division
(Directorate of Engineering Standards, ASNXD)
Wright-Patterson AFB, Ohio
Ext. 37103, 37104

NAVY: Bureau of Naval Weapons
(Aircraft Development Office, RA–14)
Washington 25, D. C.
OX 62640 or OX 67401

ARMY: Headquarters, Army Materiel Command
Washington 25, D. C.
OX 73495 or OX 57251

(1) The designated Air Force single point of contact will be the official assignment agency for the DOD.

(2) The designated Army and Navy single points of contact will be the official requesting agencies for their respective departments.

8. BLOCK NUMBER.

a. The production block number will be used to show normal production changes affecting the aircraft design and/or installed equipment. The block numbering system will consist of the assignment of production blocks, starting at 05 and progressing in multiples of five. Intermediate block numbers will be reserved for assignment by Air Materiel Command as considered necessary.

b. As many changes as possible will be accumulated for release in a production block to insure that as many aircraft as possible will be of a standard configuration.

9. YEAR OF PROCUREMENT.

This designation will be assigned to an aircraft upon manufacture and will consist of the last two digits of the fiscal year in which the procurement for that specific aircraft was authorized. This number will be will be applied to each aircraft immediately preceding the serial number.

10. SERIAL NUMBER.

The serial number of an aircraft will represent the sequential number from a block of numbers assigned to a specific type and model of aircraft when the contract for that aircraft is let. Sequence of numbers will be maintained with reference to the total procurement of aircraft and guided missiles authorized from a specific fiscal year. Aircraft of a specific type and model procured from the same or a subsequent fiscal year under another contract will be assigned numbers applicable to the fiscal year from which the new contract was authorized.

11. COMPONENT ASSIGNMENT LETTER.

This letter will be placed on each aircraft to denote the component to which it is assigned. Assignment will be determined by the rules established in AFR 65-110. Table III contains the authorized letters.

12. CLASSIFICATION LETTER.

a. The classification letter will indicate aircraft being used for experimentation and special test. Table IV contains classification letters authorized for use.

b. The classification letter will be placed at the immediate left of the prefix letter or the type letter if no prefix letter is applicable.

SECTION III

GUIDED MISSILES

1. COMPLETE GUIDED MISSILE DESIGNATION.

For reference purposes, complete designation of a typical guided missile is shown below:

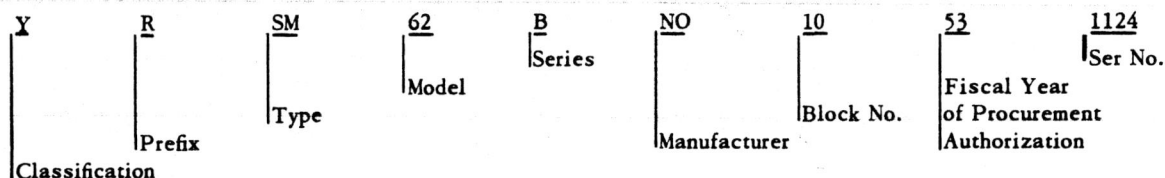

Y	R	SM	62	B	NO	10	53	1124
				Series				Ser No.
			Model				Fiscal Year	
		Type				Block No.	of Procurement	
	Prefix				Manufacturer		Authorization	
Classification								

The basic components of a missile designation, like aircraft, will consist of a type letter, model number, series letter, block number and may include prefix and/or classification letters if applicable. The general criteria established for aircraft in Figure I are applicable to missiles. Reference will be made to the text material and tables in this section in determining proper designation or redesignation of missiles.

2. TYPE LETTERS.

a. Type letters are used to denote the prime intended usage or capability of a guided missile, such as strategic, tactical, etc. Type letters will be assigned when a new missile is designed.

b. Table V contains the type letters which are approved for current usage.

3. MODEL NUMBER.

a. Model numbers are used to denote a general design of guided missile within a type.

BASIC MISSION AND TYPE SYMBOLS

Letter	Title	Description
A	Attack	Aircraft designed to search out, attack, and destroy enemy land or sea targets, using conventional or special weapons. Also used for interdiction and close air support missions.
B	Bomber	Aircraft designed for bombing enemy targets.
C	Cargo/Transport	Aircraft designed for carrying cargo and/or passengers.
E	Special Electronic Installation	Aircraft possessing ECM capability or having electronic devices to permit employment as an early warning radar station.
F	Fighter	Aircraft designed to intercept and destroy other aircraft and/or missiles.
*H	Helicopter	A rotary-wing aircraft designed with the capability of flight in any plan; e.g., horizontal, vertical, or diagonal.
K	Tanker	Aircraft designed for in-flight refueling of other aircraft.
O	Observation	Aircraft designed to observe (through visual or other means) and report tactical information concerning composition and disposition of enemy forces, troops, and supplies in an active combat area.
P	Patrol	Long range, all weather, multi-engine aircraft operating from land and/or water bases, designed for independent accomplishment of the following functions: antisubmarine warfare, maritime reconnaissance, and mining.
S	Antisubmarine	Aircraft designed to search out, detect, identify, attack, and destroy enemy submarines.
T	Trainer	Aircraft designed for training personnel in the operation of aircraft and/or related equipment, and having provisions for instructor personnel.
U	Utility	Aircraft used for miscellaneous missions such as carrying cargo and/or passengers, towing targets, etc. These aircraft include those having a small payload.
*V	VTOL and STOL	Aircraft designed for vertical take-off or landing with no take-off or landing roll, or aircraft capable of take-off and landing in a minimum prescribed distance.
X	Research	Aircraft designed for testing configurations of a radical nature. These aircraft are not normally intended for use as tactical aircraft.
*Z	Airship	A self-propelled lighter-than-air aircraft.

_____
* Type symbols

MODIFIED MISSION SYMBOLS
(PREFIX LETTERS)

Letter	Title	Description
A	Attack	Aircraft modified to search out, attack, and destroy enemy land or sea targets, using conventional or special weapons. Also used for interdiction and close air support missions.
C	Cargo/Transport	Aircraft modified for carrying cargo and/or passengers.
D	Director	Aircraft capable of controlling a drone aircraft or a missile.
E	Special Electronic Installation	Aircraft possessing ECM capability or having electronic devices to permit employment as an early warning radar station.
H	Search/Rescue	Aircraft having special equipment for performance of search and rescue missions.
K	Tanker	Aircraft having special equipment to provide in-flight refueling of other aircraft.
L	Cold Weather	Aircraft modified for operation in the arctic and antarctic regions; includes skis, special insulation, and other ancillary equipment required for extreme cold weather operations.
M	Missile Carrier	Aircraft modified for carrying and launching guided and nonguided missiles as part of the weapon system.
Q	Drone	Aircraft capable of being controlled from a point outside the aircraft.
R	Reconnaissance	Aircraft having equipment permanently installed for photographic and/or electronic reconnaissance missions.
S	Antisubmarine	Aircraft modified so that it can now function to search, identify, attack, and destroy enemy submarines.
T	Trainer	Aircraft specifically equipped or modified for training purposes.
U	Utility	Aircraft having small payload utilized or modified to perform miscellaneous missions such as carrying cargo or passengers, towing targets, etc.
V	Staff	Aircraft having accommodations such as chairs, tables, lounge, berths, etc., for the transportation of staff personnel.
W	Weather	Aircraft having meteorological equipment permanently installed.

NNN NRTTUZYUW RUWTF JA4748 1 B15124-UUUU--RUWMDTA.

ZNR UUUUU

R 241537Z APR 72

FM ATC

TO AIG 8109/LGM

RUWTEN/A/3630 FLYTNGWG SHEPPARD AFB TX/LGM

XMT LACKLAND MILTNGCEN LACKLAND AFB TX

Apr 24 17 01 72

BT

UNCLAS LGMVP

THE FOLLOWING CSAF/LGMM ALMAJCOM 838/72 IS QUOTED FOR YOUR INFORMATION AND ACTION AS NECESSARY:

"SUBJECT: TAIL MARKINS OF AIRCRAFT OVER TEN YEARS OLD. THIS MESSAGE IN FOUR PARTS. PART I FOR ALL: ATC LTR, 31 MAR 72 REQUESTED WAIVER TO PORTION OF PARA 3-20D, T.O. 1-1-4 WHICH REQUIRES THAT THE SYMBOL O- SHALL PROCEED ALL RADIO AND CALL SIGN NUMBERS ON AIRCRAFT 10 YEARS AND OLDER. AN ALL MAJ COM QUERRY BY THIS HQS REQUESTED RECOMMENDATIONS ON RETENTION OR DELE-TION. MAJCOM RESPONSES RECOMMENDED DELETION. PART 2 FOR AFLC: DELETE THAT PORTION OF REFERENCED PARAGRAPH OF T.O. 1-1-4 WHICH REQUIRES THE SYMBOL O- TO PROCEED ALL RADIO CALL SIGN NUMBERS ON ACF 10 YEARS OLD AND OLDER. PART 3 FOR ALL: REMOVAL OF SUBJECT SYMBOL WILL BE PERFORMED DURING ROUTINE SCHEDULED CORROSION/PAINT PERIODS

PAGE 2 RUWTF JA4748 UNCLAS

TO PRECLUDE UNNECESSARY MANHOUR/MATERIAL EXPENDITURES. PART 4 FOR ATC: THIS CONSTITUTES CLOSING ACTION ON YOUR REQUEST FOR WAIVER."

BT

4748

MIL-I-6140A(ASG)

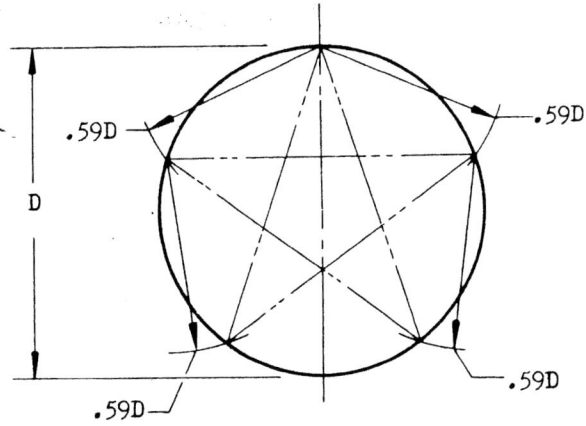

SUGGESTED CONSTRUCTION FOR TEMPLATES OR STENCILS

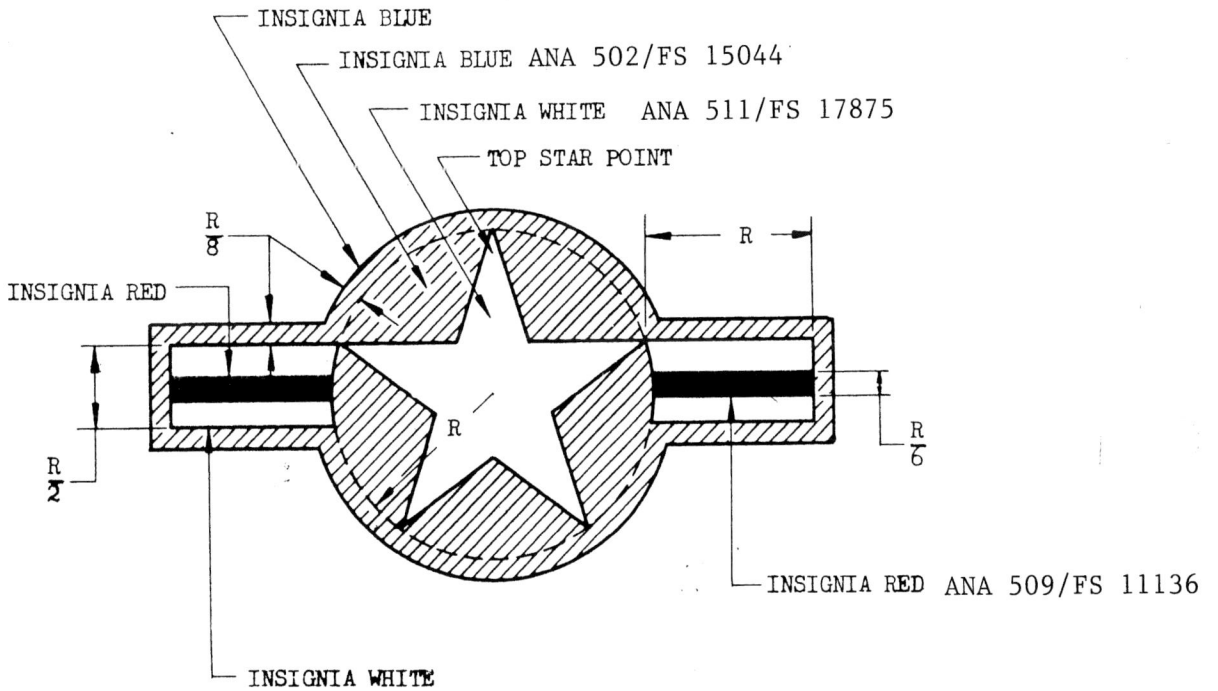

FIGURE 1. National star insignia

SR—2f
APPENDIX I.

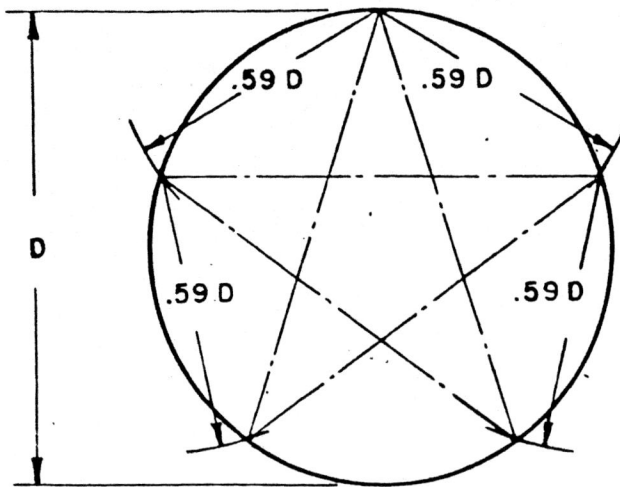

.59 D   .59 D

D

.59 D   .59 D

SUGGESTED CONSTRUCTION FOR TEMPLATES OR STENCILS

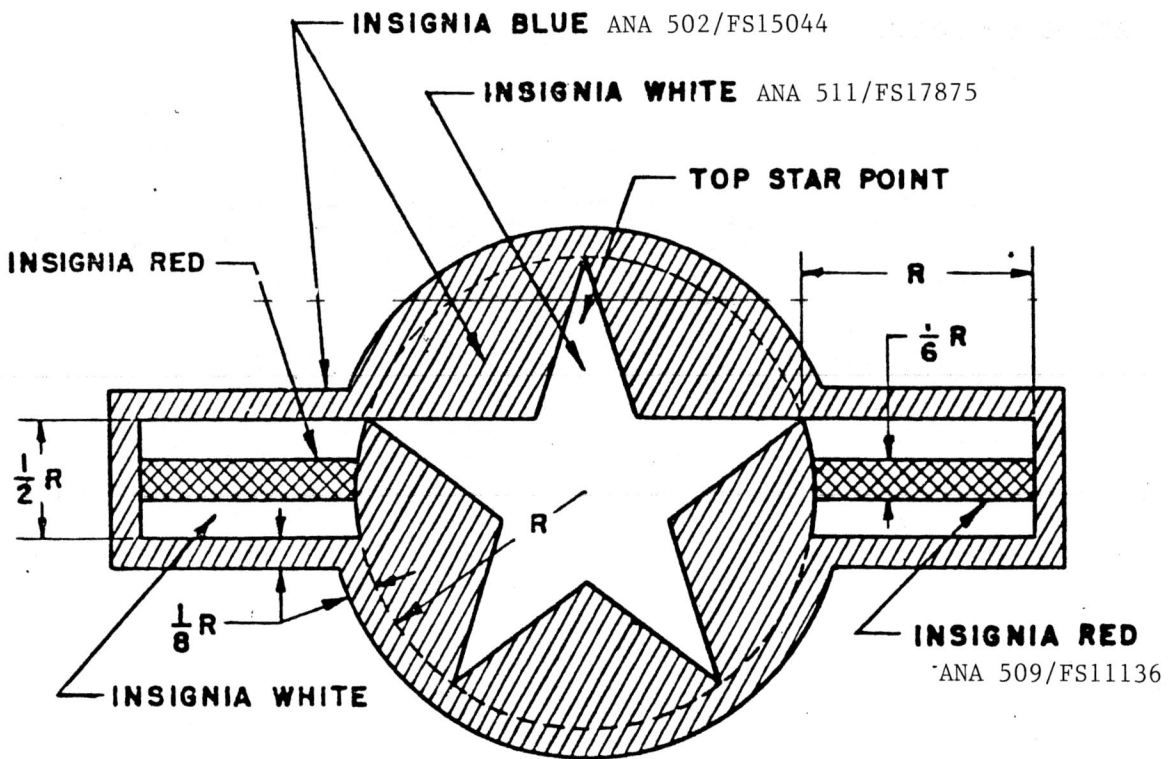

INSIGNIA BLUE ANA 502/FS15044

INSIGNIA WHITE ANA 511/FS17875

TOP STAR POINT

INSIGNIA RED

R

$\frac{1}{6}$ R

$\frac{1}{2}$ R

R

$\frac{1}{8}$ R

INSIGNIA RED
ANA 509/FS11136

INSIGNIA WHITE

NATIONAL AIRCRAFT INSIGNIA

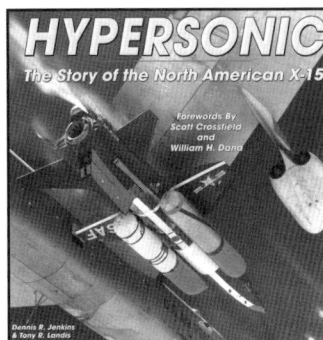

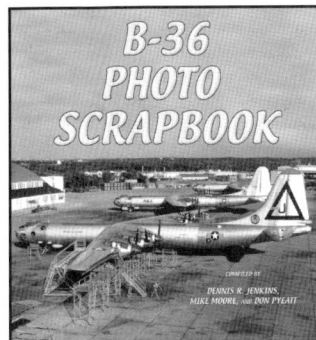

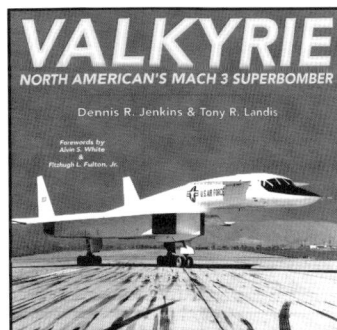

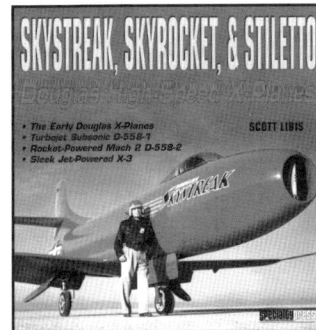

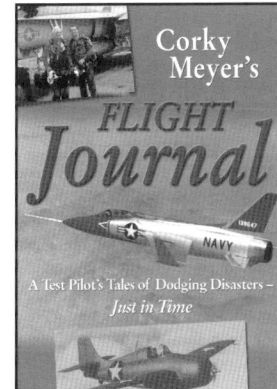

BUZZ NUMBERS

The Explanations and Regulations Behind America's Military Aircraft Identification System

After V-E Day in May 1945, many Eighth Air Force pilots engaged in unauthorized low level flying over war-ravaged Europe. This practice, called "buzzing," resulted in a need for ground observers to identify and report a particular offending aircraft. The system used two letters and three numbers, painted as large as possible on each side of the fuselage and on the underside of the left wing. The two-letter code identified the type and model of the aircraft, and the three digits include the last three numbers of the serial number.

This led to the famous "Buzz Number" system, the identification system for U.S. Army and U.S. Air Force aircraft from late 1945 into the mid-1960s. It was a combination of two preceding identification systems, one of which is still in use.

This book includes an in-depth explanation of the Buzz Number system as well as its many applications. This book is the ultimate Buzz Number reference for modelers and aviation enthusiasts.

U.S. $16.95

ISBN 1-58007-103-1

5 1695

9 781580 071031

specialtypress
PUBLISHERS AND WHOLESALERS

39966 Grand Avenue
North Branch, MN 55056 USA
(651) 277-1400 / (800) 895-4585
http://www.specialtypress.com

Distributed in the UK and Europe by
Midland Publishing

Printed in China

ITEM SP103

6 19051 00103 6

EFFECTIVE NOOM DIET MEAL PLAN

NOOM *Diet* COOKBOOK

& RECIPES TO IMPROVE METABOLISM AND LOSE WEIGHT

Christine Ensminger